THE BAY OF
Bengal

THE NEXT BRICS ASSET CLASS

T0319552

To the memory of my parents,
Soma and Ranajit

THE BAY OF
Bengal

THE NEXT BRICS ASSET CLASS

SOURAJIT AIYER

sussex
ACADEMIC
PRESS
Brighton • Chicago • Toronto

2 4 6 8 10 9 7 5 3 1

First published in Great Britain in 2018 by
SUSSEX ACADEMIC PRESS
PO Box 139, Eastbourne BN24 9BP

Distributed in North America by
SUSSEX ACADEMIC PRESS
Independent Publishers Group
814 N. Franklin Street
Chicago, IL 60610

British Library Cataloguing in Publication Data
A CIP catalogue record for this book is available from the British Library.

Library of Congress Cataloging-in-Publication Data
Names: Aiyer, Sourajit, author.
Title: The Bay of Bengal : the next BRICs asset class / Sourajit Aiyer.
Description: Brighton ; Portland : Sussex Academic Press, [2018] | Includes bibliographical references and index.
Identifiers: LCCN 2018021531 | ISBN 9781845199449 (pbk : alk. paper)
Subjects: LCSH: Economic development—Bengal, Bay of, Region. | Investments, Foreign—Bengal, Bay of, Region. | Bengal, Bay of, Region—Foreign economic relations. | Bengal, Bay of, Region—Commerce.
Classification: LCC HC430.6 .A689 2018 | DDC 330.9182/4—dc23
LC record available at https://lccn.loc.gov/2018021531

Typeset & designed by Sussex Academic Press, Brighton & Eastbourne.
Printed by TJ International, Padstow, Cornwall.

Contents

Abbreviations

Africa (Big Economies) – South Africa, Nigeria, Egypt, Morocco, Ethiopia, Kenya, Tanzania, Ghana (excludes the predominant oil economies of Sudan, Algeria and Angola)
(Economic comparisons* include all the above-mentioned countries. Corporate comparisons** exclude Ethiopia and Ghana due to data unavailability)

APAC – Asia Pacific

ASEAN – The Philippines, Thailand, Indonesia, Malaysia, Vietnam, Singapore, Laos, Cambodia, Myanmar and Brunei
(Economic comparisons include all the above-mentioned countries. Corporate comparisons exclude Malaysia, Laos, Brunei, Cambodia and Myanmar)

Bay of Bengal – India, Thailand, Bangladesh, Indonesia, Sri Lanka, Vietnam, Myanmar, Nepal and Bhutan
(Economic comparisons include all the above-mentioned countries. Corporate comparisons exclude Myanmar, Nepal and Bhutan)

BIMSTEC – India, Thailand, Bangladesh, Sri Lanka, Myanmar, Nepal and Bhutan
(Economic comparisons include all the above-mentioned countries. Corporate comparisons exclude Myanmar, Nepal and Bhutan)

BRICS – Brazil, Russia, India, China and South Africa
(Economic and corporate comparisons include all the above-mentioned countries)

BRIC – Brazil, Russia, India and China

ABBREVIATIONS

CAGR – Compounded average growth rate

CIA – Central Intelligence Agency

CIVETS – Colombia, Indonesia, Vietnam, Egypt, Turkey and South Africa
(Economic and corporate comparisons include all the above-mentioned countries)

East Africa – Kenya, Tanzania, Rwanda, Uganda, Burundi and Ethiopia
(Economic comparisons include all the above-mentioned countries. Corporate comparisons exclude Rwanda, Uganda and Burundi). Also note Ethiopia is not part of the East African Council, the regional economic bloc, but is included here as it is a dynamic economy in Eastern Africa

East Europe – Russia, Hungary, Czech Republic, Romania, Poland, Ukraine, Belarus, Moldova, Slovakia, Slovenia, Serbia, Bosnia, Croatia, Albania, Macedonia, Montenegro, Lithuania, Latvia, Estonia, Bulgaria, Georgia, Armenia and Azerbaijan
(Economic comparisons include all the above-mentioned countries. Not included in corporate comparisons)

ETF – Exchange traded fund

EXIM – Export Import Bank of India

GCC – Saudi Arabia, UAE, Qatar, Oman, Kuwait and Bahrain
(Economic comparisons include all the above-mentioned countries. Corporate comparisons exclude Bahrain)

GDP – Gross Domestic Product

ILO – International Labour Organisation

IMF – International Monetary Fund

MENA – Egypt, Morocco, Sudan, Algeria, Jordan, Iran, Iraq, Saudi Arabia, USA, Qatar, Oman, Kuwait, Bahrain and Israel
(Economic comparisons include all the above-mentioned countries. Corporate comparisons exclude Sudan, Algeria, Jordan, Iran, Iraq and Bahrain)

MHRD – Ministry of Human Resources Development

MINT – Economic and corporate comparisons include Mexico, Indonesia, Nigeria and Turkey
(Economic and corporate comparisons include all the above-mentioned countries)

MSCI EM Index – MSCI Emerging Markets Index; Chile, Colombia, India, China, Malaysia, South Korea, Taiwan, The Philippines, Thailand, Poland, South Africa, Russia, Egypt, Indonesia, Mexico, Nigeria, Pakistan, Turkey, UAE, Qatar, Hungary, Greece, Czech Republic and Peru
(Economic comparisons include all the above-mentioned countries. Corporate comparisons exclude Peru, Malaysia, Taiwan, Poland, Greece, Czech Republic and Hungary)

NEXT 11 – Bangladesh, Egypt, Indonesia, Iran, Mexico, Nigeria, Pakistan, The Philippines, Turkey, South Korea and Vietnam
(Economic comparisons include all the above-mentioned countries. Corporate comparisons exclude Iran)

PPP – Purchasing Power Parity

PSE – Public sector enterprises

RERA – Real Estate (Regulation and Development) Act, 2016

ROE – Return on equity

Rs. – Indian Rupees

Russia and CIS – Russia, Ukraine, Belarus, Moldova, Lithuania, Latvia, Estonia, Georgia, Armenia, Azerbaijan, Kazakhstan, Uzbekistan, Kyrgyz Republic, Turkmenistan and Tajikistan
(Economic comparisons include all the above-mentioned countries. Does not include corporate comparisons)

RVC – Regional value chains

ABBREVIATIONS

SAARC – India, Pakistan, Bangladesh, Maldives, Sri Lanka, Afghanistan, Nepal and Bhutan
(Economic comparisons include all the above-mentioned countries. Corporate comparisons exclude Maldives, Afghanistan, Nepal and Bhutan)

SEWA – Self Employed Women's Association

Pacific Alliance – Mexico, Chile, Colombia and Peru
(Economic comparisons include all the above-mentioned countries. Corporate comparisons exclude Peru)

UAE – United Arab Emirates

UK – United Kingdom

USA – United States of America

US$ – American Dollar

WEO – World Economic Outlook (IMF Publication)

WFE – World Federation of Exchanges

WITS – World Integrated Trade Solutions (World Bank Publication)

YoY – Year on year

* Economic data refers to all the economic metrics like GDP, per capita, savings, investments, population, etc.

** Corporate data refers to financial information of the companies like ROE, profit, revenue, debt, etc.

Disclaimer

This book is written in personal capacity, and all views expressed are personal. It should not be taken to represent those of any other organisation whatsoever. The chapter texts have been written for information purposes only, and do not construe to be an investment advice. Readers should rely on their own investigations before taking any investment action; and any such action taken by the readers would be their responsibility alone, not of the author. The book uses third-party sources for economic metrics and projections, and actual performance may vary.

Introduction

Narendra Modi and Lloyd Blankfein, India's Prime Minister and Goldman Sachs' chief executive respectively, help show the interplay between the financial economy and the political economy. As per an article in the Financial Times in January 2010, Lloyd Blankfein is said to have once jokingly remarked to his colleague Jim O'Neill that he should have called the BRICS acronym as cribs instead, when a few BRICS economies started facing cyclical and structural headwinds. While most economic stories are ephemeral, this highlights the critical role of the financial economy in spreading the buzz about potential groups in the first place. After all, it was Goldman Sach's Jim O'Neill who coined the term BRIC in 2001. Subsequently, the early 2000s saw several portfolio funds launched dedicated to the BRIC asset class as that buzz spread. Hence, even when the 2010s saw that interest diminish slightly as a few BRICS markets faced headwinds, the buzz pushed the political economy to take the BRIC story onto a larger canvas. BRIC expanded to BRICS. Their governments laid down the agenda for socio-economic cooperation. Since then, their agenda has progressed on pressing development issues. In the process, the efforts of the political economy have kept the BRICS story relevant even today. However, the initial trigger that created all that buzz - be it spreading the awareness of these economies, their homogeneity, moving them from being under-appreciated to well-acknowledged markets or making politicians realize that such a grouping was even conceivable, all came from the financial economy in the early 2000s. It was the low-hanging fruit that eventually helped financial practitioners look at the whole tree.

At the 2016 BRICS summit when India's Prime Minister Narendra Modi extended the invite to BIMSTEC, a group of countries around the Bay of Bengal sea, he re-asserted the commitment of the political economy for cooperation within this group. But there still exists a veritable gap in the financial economy's appreciation of this group, something that helped make BRICS the brand that it is today. As a result, the financial economy is not yet complementing the political economy's efforts in BIMSTEC.

The objective of this book

The Bay of Bengal markets suffer from a lack of popular buzz. Reversing the lack of awareness is essential to create that buzz, so that the financial economy and political economy complement each other. One way to trigger this buzz is to show the financial economy a rationale for creating an asset class on this group just like it occurred in the BRICS. That would help them see these markets as a cohesive group, and appreciate the potential, performance, homogeneity and complementarities of these economies. This is the moot objective of the book. For those who may not know, an asset class is a basket of securities exhibiting similar characteristics. The constituents have strong economic fundamentals, buoyant corporate performance and low correlation to counter the volatility of single-market exposure. BRIC became a de facto asset class since funds started investing as per that group, though it was not a traditional asset-class. In the same vein, this book talks of the Bay of Bengal markets, and the potential to create an asset class on it.

The chapters to follow take a top-down view of the Bay of Bengal markets. It shows why their drivers of economic growth (consumption, investment, net export) make a fair mix; the commonalities and complementarities of these economies; if this group's story is less ephemeral; relative profit performance vs. global peers and why this group stands out on this metric; whether the group is of a relevant size; its savings and purchasing power comparisons; their sector-mix; the impact of formalisation in deepening its businesses; and much more. The narrative stresses why it is to India's advantage to be part of this group, despite its comparatively larger size. Since no market is perfect, the book talks about the group's challenges in productivity, investment and trade, so that these factors do not impede the group in the long term. Each chapter deals with a separate theme; and they all add up to show the rationale of this grouping. Some findings show that the existent hype about some larger emerging markets doesn't always accompany substance. Unlike trade or economic blocs whose negotiations take time, a portfolio asset class group is comparatively a quicker implementation project. Such an asset class can generate investor interest in these countries as a single group. An asset class could also pave the way for Bay of Bengal-dedicated funds, just like the conception of BRIC preceded the setting up of BRIC-dedicated funds. That would make the financial markets more vibrant, which can help create a motivating ecosystem for corporates – a win for investors. For global businesses, it can be the next big marketing campaign.

The book combines data, travel-impressions and inferences. This includes my travels to Bangladesh, Sri Lanka, Indonesia, Vietnam, India, Thailand, Malaysia, Cambodia, Bhutan and Nepal between 2016 and 2018. These journeys gave me an opportunity to talk to the local people. Some anecdotes are written to provide context. The data compares various economic and financial metrics, with a focus on the two-dozen large emerging markets and neighbouring countries. Deliberation is done on the data to arrive at qualitative inferences.

The proposed Bay of Bengal group includes India, Bangladesh, Thailand, Sri Lanka, Myanmar, Nepal, Bhutan, Indonesia and Vietnam. The first seven are part of the regional group BIMSTEC, and all nine make up the book's proposed Bay of Bengal grouping. The last two countries are added because they have a similar demographic/development profile to India and enjoy friendly ties with it. Moreover, Indonesia and Vietnam have better developed financial markets than some of the smaller markets of BIMSTEC. Economic comparisons aggregate all nine markets, while financial comparisons aggregate Bangladesh, India, Thailand, Indonesia, Vietnam and Sri Lanka. Those who argue Vietnam does not touch the Bay of Bengal should know that neither do Nepal or Bhutan. In any case, the BRICS was more scattered. But with shipping lines between East Asia and Europe passing through this Bay of Bengal region, opportunities to create synergies here will be dynamic.

Two key questions

Before moving on to the chapter synopsis, it is pertinent to address two key questions that arise at this stage, i.e. is this group relevant and what are its growth-drivers?

DID YOU KNOW that this Bay of Bengal group is expected to reach the same economic size by 2021 as the BRICS did in 2006, five years after the term BRIC was coined.

That it is expected to add a similar economic size on an incremental basis as the BRICS ex China grouping, over the five years till 2021.

That the expected nominal growth rate of this group at ~9% from 2016 to 2021 is the highest amongst all major groups/acronyms of developing countries.

That it is the only group along with BRICS and ASEAN which is expected to see a combination of high savings rate, savings growth and savings size by 2021; and that many hyped groups globally (including BRICS ex China grouping) do not rank well on these aspects

That this group would also see one of the closest synchronised-growth amongst its members up to 2021, i.e. most members growing together by a similar extent.

That this group's average per-capita is already higher than what it was for the BRICS back in 2001.

That as much as 43% of all the large listed companies across a sample of seventeen major emerging/frontier markets that delivered a 10% plus return on equity (ROE) in each of the preceding five years were from this group's markets

That as many as 40% of all companies from these sample markets that delivered a 30% plus compounded average growth rate (CAGR) in profits over the last five years were from this group

That six out of the top eight markets from this sample that saw the most profitable companies in 2016 were from this group

That as many as six out of the ten markets that saw at least 40% of their companies deliver profit growth in terms of their last five-year CAGR, were from this group

That within this group itself as much as 34% of its large listed companies delivered a 10% plus ROE in each of the preceding five years, same as the BRICS

That the profit pool of its markets balances a fair mix of manufacturing and services

And did you know it extends the basket's profit exposure to consumer and industrials, two sectors which grow in relevance as markets mature?

All these data and much more are discussed in the book. These probably capture a group's relevance better than simply quoting its proportion to global gross domestic product (GDP) or population, as is often done in the case of the BRICS. Even on these two standard metrics, the share of the Bay of Bengal group to global GDP at ~6% in 2016 was similar to that of the BRICS ex China group, despite being only half of it a decade ago. Also, the group formed ~27% of global population in 2016, much higher than BRICS ex China's 23%.

The second question is about the group's economic growth-drivers. Expectations about BRICS ex China & India (i.e. Brazil, South Africa and Russia) leaned heavily on the commodity trade cycle, which did not sustain. A revival in the prices of certain commodities in recent months, as of writing in May 2018, may have brought back some interest, though structural challenges in those economies still persist. Their gross invest-ment rates remain low, and their low savings rate force external borrowings. Any revival only seems temporary. Despite this, over 3,000 global funds continued to have over 90% allocation to Brazil, which is ~3x of that to India or South Korea, as of early 2017 based on Bloomberg data. Do their fundamentals merit that investor interest?

This is where the Bay of Bengal grouping stands out. Its group countries have a fair mix of economic growth-drivers across consumption, invest-ment and net exports. Its group countries like Thailand and Indonesia were strong exporters traditionally. The last five years also saw high export growth in Bangladesh and Vietnam. Bangladesh is the only South Asian nation to have a current account surplus. In the next five years, Bangladesh may see consumption pick up, while Vietnam is expected to maintain its export momentum. India, Thailand and Indonesia, along with Myanmar and Bhutan, are expected to see traction in exports. In the last five years, imports grew in Bangladesh, Vietnam, Sri Lanka, Indonesia and Myanmar, which coincides with a growth in their investment rate, indi-cating productive asset-creation. This has been sluggish in India. The expectation till 2021 is that the average investment rate will pick up in Bangladesh and Nepal, while the others will maintain it. Most of the nine countries will see investment growing slightly higher than nominal GDP on a CAGR basis till 2021. This investment rate may slip in India till 2021, which is a challenge. Savings have been strong in most of the group's countries, and are expected to remain so. Much of the investment growth in the group so far has been backed by domestic savings, mini-mizing external borrowings. Again, the exception is India where, despite having sizable savings, the savings rate has slipped in its consumption frenzy. Along with Bangladesh, Thailand and Indonesia are expected to see strong domestic consumption, critical in nations of their population size. Consumption has been the leading story in India, and further deepening of its middle-class should keep up the momentum. Even the smaller markets are expected to see strong consumption. Despite this, inflation in these countries has not been as high as in some of the more prominent emerging markets. If one looks at Okun's Misery Index, it is below 10% for most of the group's countries, unlike some large emerging markets. The chapter on Asset Class will discuss all these growth-drivers further with data.

The range of the per-capita income of the countries in this group is less than the ASEAN, implying relatively less heterogeneity in the group's profile. The ASEAN as a whole ranks well on growth and savings, but the economic profile of the grouping has become more heterogeneous with Malaysia, Singapore and Brunei reaching a different stage than Laos, Cambodia or Myanmar. This implies different priorities. The economies in the Bay of Bengal group are homogeneously closer. This mix should help them complement each other to maintain the group's overall growth even if one driver stumbles, while minimizing the chance of repeating a crisis like the BRICS of 2010s or the ASEAN of 1997.

Chapter synopsis

The Asset Class chapter looks at the commonalities of this group in terms of its economic construct, portfolio construct and equity markets construct to create the initial awareness of this group. It looks at the linearity and synchronisation of growth across the group's economies. Thereafter, it looks at the complementarities in the mix of its economic growth drivers across consumption, investment and export, major sector exposure in the profit-pool, and the push to deepen the domestic investor base.

The Profit chapter shows how the group's markets demonstrated better fundamental performance between 2012 and 2016 relative to its more-hyped peers in the emerging market universe. It looks at several data of ROE, profits, margins, productivity and leverage, in terms of the consistency in performance, improvement in performance, components of ROE as well as certain challenges that these markets face.

The Purchasing Power chapter takes a look at some of the critical components of a country's purchasing power, i.e. the stock of savings, the flow of income, the size of per capita and the distribution of money amongst the population, to see how this group's consumer base is placed on all three fronts.

The Investment chapter looks at how the various regions have ramped up their investment levels, and the extent to which it can impact economic output. It estimates the ideal investment rate seen across high-growth economies in the initial stage of their development journey. It compares if more investment has gone into investment or manufacturing, and why there is a pressing incentive for the Bay of Bengal group countries to ramp up investments right now.

The Sector chapter looks at whether certain sectors start contributing disproportionately to a market's profit pool as the economy matures, if the journey yet to be traversed offers an investment opportunity in itself, whether the mix of manufacturing and services in a single portfolio is a rationale, why larger economies still need other sectors to grow and if there is a tipping point beyond which the relative size of the companies in sectors of competitive advantage do not have a maximising impact on the overall economy any more.

The Productivity chapter shows how some broader issues can affect the long term productivity of specific sections of the workforce, especially those making up a large chunk in India. It raises two challenges that may impact the supply of productive employees, a growing disincentive to skill and shortage of critical thinking. At the same time, the near-term outlook on productivity improvement in most Bay of Bengal countries is healthy and they are expected to see both productivity and workforce addition contribute to incremental output.

The Formalisation chapter looks at the Process Technology Policy (PTP) Model to see how businesses are receiving a push from formalisation. It shows examples from the Bay of Bengal markets to show how formalisation is helping make certain business sectors more organised. At the same time, formalisation also implies changes in the way businesses are done, and investors have to be wary of these.

The Risk chapter evaluates the risks of doing and the risks of not doing something. It looks at risks from the perspective of the Bay of Bengal markets, especially the case of India where being part of a group portfolio in its current scenario of high leverage and slippage in investment/savings may help mitigate the perception of the risk of a group portfolio vs. that of a singular exposure, to some extent.

The Integration chapter explains that while regional financial integration can be an enabler, it is not a compulsion for a group asset class idea. However, the grouping may yet gain if business integration is pushed through regional value chains (RVC) and even production migration. Lastly, geographical proximity is not a compulsion either for a group asset class idea, if one compares the success of BRICS and ASEAN on this front.

The Trade chapter studies if intra-regional trade contributed towards the BRICS story, and demonstrates that intra-regional trade is not a necessity for a financial asset class idea. At the same time, a micro-approach with the final outcome in mind can be more beneficial, and it is critical to ensure the deepening of trade in a group does not exacerbate the deficit problem. It shows that trade relationships for India within the Bay of Bengal countries are already on a better footing as compared to the BRICS.

This group combines size and profitability

The Bay of Bengal group's equity markets combine size and profitability. India has a wide base of listed companies, next only to China and South Korea in the emerging markets; and their average size is large. It helps add the mass to the group in terms of the scale of opportunities that could absorb investment. At the same time, the Southeast and the other South Asian countries in the group delivered better fundamentals relative to India, in terms of profit margins or ROE over the last five years. They have lower levels of leverage than India, indicating headroom for further growth. Their markets add more profitable (investible) opportunities to the group that could absorb investment. Investments are still made into the individual stocks. However, the basket has an advantage from the perspective of how fund managers view these markets as a portfolio group. The average allocation in a BRIC-dedicated fund to India has been ~15%, much higher than its ~2–4% allocation in a typical emerging market fund or an Asia ex Japan fund. The Bay of Bengal portfolio might see similar outcomes.

Are acronyms passé

Acronyms are becoming passé in investing parlance because many markets did not sustain their expectations. However, they still stay on like an unwanted room-mate. You dislike them, yet you need them as they help spread out the rent, and reduce that risk for each individual. While any new acronym will be looked upon as hype, one still needs them because the stories of individual markets are becoming volatile. This is due to continued overdependence on cycles, inability to enact reforms, structural deficiencies or inability to compete with the countries that have entered the global bandwagon. Putting all monies in a portfolio with exposure to a singular market is risky. One can still invest the same amount in one market, but it may be wise to spread it across diversified portfolios so that the downside risk of the portfolio is cushioned if that one market hits headwinds. Of course, it also means capping the upside in case that one market turns out to be a winner, but data shows a tricky picture on this. As per the IMF's World Economic Outlook (WEO) data, only one-third of all countries globally clocked a higher growth rate in 2015 than the previous year. This was as high as two-thirds back in 2000. And in many cases, analysts often cannot estimate correctly which these would be.

Even the political economy will drive acronyms. Growth is getting redistributed with several developing countries entering the global production value-chain. While each country wants a share in this pie, globalisation thrives on competitiveness and every nation cannot be equally competitive at the same time. Countries can end up with better prospects by aligning themselves into a group due to the synergies it offers. This will continue to drive the need for alliances to converge interests in geopolitics, trade and investments. Also, new alliances will come up to substitute the less successful ones. For instance, BIMSTEC itself is touted as a more workable substitute to SAARC. At the same time, developing countries that investors do not categorise into popular acronyms are improving. During a trip to Bangladesh in 2017 after a gap of 12 years, I saw significant improvements in its streets and civic services, especially in northern Dhaka where businessman turned mayor, Annisul Huq, played a key role. Yes, much is still left to be done and Mayor Huq's demise was unfortunate. Nonetheless, it is a degree of positive transformation that has improved the productivity of people. With many under-hyped countries improving, merit is a reason for combining them into groups.

In conclusion, the political economy is setting the agenda of BIMSTEC on critical fronts. But these are long-gestation projects. In the BRICS, intra-group trade cooperation is yet to take off in a big way even now, more than fifteen years after the conceptualisation of BRIC by Goldman Sachs. However, the BRICS of the 2000s shows that creating and sustaining the buzz is important, so that the financial economy appreciates the potential of a grouping and conceives a portfolio asset class idea on that group, which in turn, can help till the longer-gestation projects of the political economy rolled out. Can the Bay of Bengal group repeat this? We shall see by looking at several aspects of this group's markets to help deepen the awareness and appreciation of the financial community. That can help create the buzz, and set off the chain of events like in the BRICS. If anything, it can start off as the next big marketing campaign for global sellers, just like the BRICS did.

This part of the world remains a complex market to do business in. Unlike the West where the formal rules of law provide collateral, relationship-based management provides better collateral here since the formal rules of law are still evolving. Local businesses who understand these nuances deliver better financial results. So it may be better to invest through these businesses if one wants to have exposure to these markets. A portfolio asset class idea for this group helps towards that objective.

Commonalities and Complementarities
The Asset Class Story

In 2016, while attending a South Asian industry conference in Nepal to give a presentation, a delegation from China's Belt and Road Initiative also happened to visit the same hotel for an event of their own. They were in Nepal to pitch their mega Belt and Road investment project to Nepal's government and businesses. Some of us were asked if we would be interested to meet the Chinese delegation, to make use of the chance that they were in the same hotel. During informal conversation with the Chinese delegates, it was interesting to hear their views about how to pitch a foreign investment proposal effectively. Their view was to start with the commonalities to entice the audience initially, and then move on to the complementarities to induce the action – always in that order. Commonalities must be pitched upfront to get the audience interested in a noisy world. This is more so because the level of awareness of the current generation, including amongst many business and investment professionals, about the regional Asian economies, is still quite low. That is a paradox since this generation has access to a large information overload, yet most of that is probably just financial noise and theatre.

Pitching of commonalities upfront helps bridge that awareness gap, while not seen to be pushy from the word go. Call it creating a sense of common identity or simply enticing to get them interested to listen more; it helps get a foot in the door. However, the idea is not only to make one listen, but to make them act as well. So complementary has to follow commonality. Inducing that action helps close the deal on the ground. Complementarities help give substantiated answers to those critics who question whether the proposal is a fair deal. If complementarities are pitched ahead of commonalities, then that initial foundation of mutual awareness and appreciation may not get created, which may be detrimental in the long term for sustaining support for the project. The action always takes longer and so it is important that support is sustained. That is where sticking to this order helps, and it has helped them convert proposals in various countries.

The BRICS story also evolved as an asset class in a similar manner. BRIC started out with Goldman Sachs talking about the commonalities between the four economies (South Africa was added later). These commonalities included talking about their size, expected growths, contribution to the global pie, etc. It helped generate initial interest in these countries, which is a precedent for an asset class story. That set the ball rolling and the global community became more aware about these markets and started appreciating their potential.

After pitching the commonalities, the story then moved to complementarities in areas like trade. For instance, China as a growing manufacturing powerhouse wanted endless supply of commodities. Countries like Brazil, South Africa and Russia were major exporters of commodities and complemented that demand. Thus, the talk of the commodity export super-cycle was born as one of the selling-points of the BRICS story, especially from Brazil, Russia and South Africa to China (China's imports were over 40% of intra-BRICS import volumes over the last decade, as per the data in EXIM Bank of India's report 'Intra-BRICS trade: An Indian Perspective'). Pitching commonalities upfront also helped create the BRICS portfolio asset class, wherein the individual markets complemented each other to create an upside for the group as a whole. As a result, a plethora of BRIC-dedicated portfolio funds came up from the 2000s onwards.

It is a different story that the commodity cycle did not sustain. Many of those portfolio funds lost sheen as cyclical and structural challenges hit three BRICS countries; in fact the Goldman Sachs BRICS portfolio was merged with their broader emerging market fund. Nevertheless it helped take the story ahead amongst the financial community through the 2000s. As the political economy now takes forward the BRICS agenda on a broader canvas of socio-economic development, they maintain that focus on searching for complementarities. So it started with commonalities followed by complementarities in the BRICS, just like the Chinese delegates opined in the case of their Belt and Road Initiative.

Putting the same approach on the Bay of Bengal group, does it help convey its rationale as a portfolio asset class? Is it an effective approach to present the underlying rationale for a proposal?

Starting with commonalities

The portfolio's construct

On a typical financial asset-class 3*3 matrix which differentiates securities on the basis of capitalisation (large, mid and small caps) or type of investment (growth or value), an asset class idea on the Bay of Bengal markets would probably have a bias on the long term value box and the mid cap box across most of its markets. The mid cap bias is in view of the average size of the listed companies in most of the group's markets, except possibly Thailand and India. The value bias is in view of the stage of the economic evolution in most of these markets, which creates a long term opportunity for many businesses to go deeper and grow further. The Bay of Bengal markets combine a mix of size and profitability when it comes to its equity markets. India has a wide base of listed companies, and the average size of its companies is larger than most other markets. It helps add the mass of opportunities that could absorb investment. The Southeast and South Asian markets in the group have better fundamentals relative to India. They add more investible opportunities.

So not only are these economies at a common stage of development, but these markets complement each other in this combined basket across mass and performance, and this can help from the perspective of how fund managers view these markets as a group as compared to viewing them individually. The smaller markets in the group gain by being part of a group with India which already evinces a lot of investor interest, while India gains by being part of a group that has more profitable opportunities to evince investor interest.

Such Bay of Bengal-dedicated portfolio funds could result in more inflows into its smaller markets, just like BRIC-dedicated funds helped flow more monies into India than what would have been possible otherwise. In the early 2000s when India was a relatively newly-opened market and the larger BRICS markets like China and Brazil already garnered more investor attention, single-country India funds were yet to find many takers. The BRICS funds hastened that journey towards single-country funds by spreading the awareness of this new market to the global financial community. This pace may have been slower had India only depended on the emerging market or Asia ex Japan funds, because India formed a smaller, possibly a satellite, share of their pie. The average 15% allocation to India in a BRICS fund was higher that its average 2–5% allocation in an emerging market fund or an Asia ex Japan fund (where the bulk of the allocation went to South Korea, China or Taiwan).

In the same way, portfolio funds on the Bay of Bengal group's markets can help hasten the launch of single-country funds dedicated to their individual markets. The smaller markets of the Bay of Bengal group can get a higher allocation as compared to the average sub-5% they enjoy in a typical frontier fund (where the bulk of the allocation goes to Kuwait, Nigeria or the Philippines).

The economic growth's construct

As per the IMF's WEO data projections, the gross domestic product (GDP) of the economies comprising the Bay of Bengal group are projected to collectively grow at a 9% CAGR over the next five years till 2021, the highest amongst all the popular groups and acronyms of developing nations including ASEAN, BRICS, Next 11, MINT, CIVETS, GCC, MENA, East Africa, Africa (Big Economies), East Europe, CIS, SAARC, Pacific Alliance and even the MSCI Emerging Markets Index (MSCI EM Index) grouping.

But it is more important to break up this growth to identify commonalities, rather than just look at a growth number by itself. Between 2001 and 2006, most of the BRICS countries grew their individual share to the global GDP pie, irrespective of the share of the developing countries or emerging markets as a whole. In the same way, between 2016 and 2021, most of the Bay of Bengal countries are expected to grow their individual share to the global pie, irrespective of the share of the developing countries or emerging markets as a whole – India from 3% to 3.6%, Thailand from 0.5%

to 0.6%, Bangladesh from 0.3% to 0.4%, Indonesia from 1.2% to 1.5%, Vietnam from 0.27% to 0.31%, Sri Lanka from 0.1% to 0.11%, Myanmar from 0.08% to 0.10%, etc.

Looking at GDP by Purchasing Power Parity (PPP) method, often deemed a better measure for relative comparison between countries, the CAGR in GDP (PPP) has been in the range of 5–10% during the last five years up to 2016 for almost all the individual countries making up the Bay of Bengal group. In the same way, the CAGR had been in the range of 5–10% for almost all the individual countries making up the BRIC for the five years up to 2001.

Most importantly, the Bay of Bengal markets share a high degree of synchronisation and linearity amongst the growth-trajectories of the individual markets from now till 2021. This means that most of the markets are expected to grow at a similar track, and there are no major outliers. In comparison, the BRICS has severe outliers because the growth trajectory in South Africa, Russia and Brazil has widely diverged from that of China and India in recent years. This commonality in the synchronised growth and linearity in the growth journey is a critical driver to regarding these markets as a single, cohesive group.

Investors dislike volatility in a market's growth trend, because it brings in uncertainties in the outlook at that point of time. After all, nobody likes negative surprises. If one looks at the standard deviation of the year on year (YoY) growth rates of these groups till 2021 as a simple measure of the linearity in their projected growth trend, then the highest degree of volatility between 2–5% can be seen in regions like the BRICS ex China grouping, Russia & CIS, East Europe, MINT and Africa (Big Economies). Conversely, the least volatility between 0–1% is seen in regions like East Africa, MENA, BIMSTEC ex India, SAARC ex India and BRICS.

Regions like Bay of Bengal, BIMSTEC, ASEAN, Next 11, CIVETS, SAARC, Pacific Alliance, GCC and even the MSCI EM Index all lie in between. A reason for ASEAN might be the existence of constituents that are varied across the development chart. For example, Singapore, Brunei and Malaysia in ASEAN are low-population and high-income nations that have reached a reasonable level of development, and they will grow at a steady-state in line with most of the other matured economies across the globe.

Conversely, Laos, Myanmar, Vietnam and Cambodia are low-income countries that are opening up their economies and opportunities abound. They suffer from a shortage of investment and the fulfilment of this should result in high rates of growth. With the South Asian economies, Bhutan and Sri Lanka are expected to see a sudden spurt in their growth rates after two to three years from now; herewith a reason why the Bay of Bengal group has a standard deviation not far from 1%. If the developed markets serve as a benchmark, then the combined expected growth of the five developed economies of USA, UK, Germany, Canada and Japan has a volatility of ~0.7%.

Linearity aside, is this growth synchronised across most of the group economies? Synchronised growth can be called a misnomer at times, because the chance of all the countries in a group moving in the same direction throughout the period is very rare in reality, irrespective of estimations. A look at the BRICS experience in the late-1990s is revealing, when its story gained popularity with the Goldman Sachs note published in 2001. The historical GDP growth of the BRICS countries during the years from 1996 to 2002 does not show any semblance of synchronised growth whatsoever. Only China and India moved together in line in an upward slope, with CAGRs of 9% and 4% for the five-year period from 1996 to 2001. The remaining three – Brazil, Russia and South Africa - all lagged with de-growths of -8%, -5% and -4% respectively. Of course, South Africa was not part of the original term coined in 2001, but removing it does not make the picture any better. The overall CAGR for BRICS as a whole was a mere 1% for that period.

Yet from 2001 onwards, the BRICS story became the bedrock for rolling out several BRIC-dedicated portfolio funds. This was because the expectation was far removed from the historical trend, and the BRICS markets did deliver. The combined BRICS economy grew at a CAGR of 17% from 2001 to 2006, with every group economy contributing. Synchronised growth still offers a look into the commonalities of the expected growth journey of the constituents of that group. After all, if the constituents are not expected to move together in projections, then there is less chance they will do so in reality. If projected data expects the constituents to move together, one assumes there may still be a slim chance that they might do so to some extent in reality.

Using the IMF's WEO data projections, the growth trends expected till 2021 in the individual countries within these groups show that only the Bay of Bengal, BIMSTEC, Next 11 and ASEAN groups will have more than 50% of their underlying constituents growing at a CAGR that is above the CAGR for that combined region. To explain this simply, it means that if the CAGR of the combined GDP of the countries making up a group is x%, then at least 50% of the constituents of that group are expected to grow at a CAGR above or equal to x%. These four groups cross the 50% mark. Others like MINT, MENA, East Africa and Africa (Big Economies), all notch exactly 50%. The other groups like BRICS, East Europe and Pacific Alliance have less than half of their constituents expected to grow above the group's combined growth figure. To use a benchmark, the MSCI EM Index has only 42% of its constituents expected to cross the group's combined growth. This may not be encouraging if an investor is looking at the group as a potential investment. If only a few countries within the group will grow together, then one is better off looking at them singularly. If synchronised growth of the maximum constituents in the group has any worth, then the Bay of Bengal group scores a point here.

In absolute size, the Bay of Bengal group is expected to comprise a similar economic size (approximately US$6 billion) by 2021. This is the same as the BRICS back in 2006, five years after the term BRIC was coined. The contribution of BRICS ex China grouping was 11% of the incremental global GDP (addition to GDP) for the five-years from 2001 to 2006, and will be a similar 10% of the incremental global GDP for the next five years till 2021. In the same way, the contribution of the Bay of Bengal is expected to be 10% of the incremental global GDP till 2021, quite close to the numbers clocked by the BRICS ex China grouping.

The famous Okun Misery Index of Arthur Okun is a useful measure of the state of worries of any economy, as it combines unemployment and infla-tion. This is below 10% currently in most of the Bay of Bengal countries, while it is much higher for some of the BRICS ex China and the larger emerging markets.

A number of comparisons here have been done on an ex China basis, like BRICS ex China, because the Chinese engine became disproportionately large relative to the other countries. Even though China has slowed down from the near double-digit growth rates of the 2000s, it is still adding the equivalent of several countries each year. So any number of the group of which it is a part becomes skewed. The idea of seeing the figure on an ex China basis is to understand how the other countries fared after removing the extent of skewness. Similarly, some other regions have also been compared by removing one disproportionately large member, like East Europe ex Russia or BIMSTEC ex India, etc.

Lastly, while the methodology of Ease of Doing Business rankings may have its own shortcomings, most of the Bay of Bengal markets have improved substantially in recent years. In the last two years, Indonesia improved by 37 places. India improved by 30 places. Thailand and Vietnam also improved by 20-odd places each.

The equity markets' construct

ROE and its components as per the Du-Pont method are one of the best barometers of an equity market's fundamental performance. If one looks at the Bloomberg data of the largest 200 listed companies of each market as per 2016 market capitalisation, then the ROE of the individual BRICS countries varies significantly. For instance, the average ROE of the last five years up to 2016 was ~14–15% in China and India while it was ~8–10% in Russia and Brazil, as per Bloomberg. Such variance can impact the risk of the portfolio, since the downside of one severely limits the upside from another. YoY comparison between countries may have limitations due to differing year-ends, but the idea is only to get an indication. Conversely, the last five-year average ROEs in most of the Bay of Bengal group countries (i.e. only India, Thailand, Bangladesh, Sri Lanka, Indonesia and Vietnam since their listed company financial data was available) was bunched around the 13–14% range. Vietnam at ~10% was the only exception. This can protect the downside pressure on the portfolio to some extent. ROE is discussed further in the chapter on Profit.

So while the average size of this group's markets may be smaller than the BRICS markets (average profit per company of the largest 200 companies in 2016 was ~$278 million in India, ~$122 million in Thailand, ~$95 million in Indonesia, ~$11 million in Bangladesh, ~$8 million in Sri Lanka and ~$3 million in Vietnam as compared to ~$1751 million in China, ~$180 million in Brazil, ~$327 million in Russia and ~$144 million in South Africa), they delivered better ROEs. Incidentally, Indonesia's average profit per company was similar to emerging markets like Turkey, Saudi Arabia and the United Arab Emirates (UAE). In terms of the size of market capitalisation, the average market capitalisation across the BRICS markets was in the range of US$150 billion back in 2001. Assuming this range to be a threshold to entice fund manager interest in emerging market stories, the average across the Bay of Bengal grouping (excluding India) exceeds this threshold. Adding India takes it further north.

At the same time, if one looks at the number of listed companies available as the potential canvas available to any investor, then the smaller markets of the Bay of Bengal group have more listed companies than Brazil and Russia do even today. The number of listed companies in any market is not really a yardstick because it really depends on the investible opportunities. Hence, the breadth of the companies that delivered profit growth over the last five years may be a better yardstick. After all, profit growth is a fundamental metric any investor looks at. According to this method, the percentage of the largest 200 companies in each market that saw a positive CAGR in their profits from 2011 to 2016 was about 50% for the Bay of Bengal group as a whole, including BIMSTEC (55% in Sri Lanka, 54% in Bangladesh, 53% in India, 49% in Thailand, 44% in Vietnam and 42% in Indonesia). In comparison, this was 40% in BRICS as a whole, 46% in ASEAN, 40% in MENA and GCC each, 34% in MINT, 36% in East Africa, 31% in Africa (Big Economies) and 27% in Pacific Alliance. For the MSCI EM Index as a whole, this was 38%. In fact, the Bay of Bengal markets scored ahead than larger emerging markets like Brazil, Russia, South Africa, Nigeria, Turkey, Saudi Arabia or Mexico.

The average debt to equity level of the largest 200 companies in each of the Bay of Bengal markets, except India, ranges between 0.7x to 1x. This offers ample headroom to fund future growth.

During the 1997 Asian currency crisis, most of the Southeast Asian countries made investments to push their export sectors and ended up with significant external borrowings since their domestic savings were not enough back then. Does the Bay of Bengal risk such an occurrence? Chances are slim, since most of this group's economies are high savings countries, both from savings rate and savings size. With a large portion of investments being funded by these sizable savings, the risk of running up excess external borrowings is less.

The most important commonality for the Bay of Bengal region markets, which feeds its growth estimates to some extent, is its consumption base. Between 50–70% of the GDP of most of the nine Bay of Bengal group countries are driven by consumption, with the average for the group as a whole coming to two-thirds, largely in line with the MSCI EM Index grouping. Absolute population is an incomplete measure of the consumption opportunity, nevertheless the Bay of Bengal region is home to 27% of the global population, and this share is marginally increasing each year. This is higher than the 23% of the BRICS ex China grouping. Even the BIMSTEC alone forms ~22% of global population.

BRICS comprised about 44% of the global population back in 2001. This share has decreased over the years to reach 42% in 2016, due to the impact of China's one-child policy and the flat population growth in Russia. On the other hand, the share of the population of the Bay of Bengal grouping to global population has increased marginally during this period, from 26.8% in 2001 to 27.2% in 2016. More importantly, the population is more spread out across the countries in the Bay of Bengal group than in the BRICS. More than 90% of the BRICS population was concentrated in the two mammoth countries of China and India. In the Bay of Bengal group, the two most populated nations – India and Indonesia - comprise less than 80% of the total group's population. In fact, the group's countries like Indonesia, Bangladesh and Thailand have a larger population than the BRICS nations like Brazil, Russia and South Africa, respectively.

The consumption story is one that will evince the interest of not only global investors looking at its markets, but also of businesses looking to expand. Some have already done so. Axiata is a Malaysian telecom company which has built presence across Bay of Bengal markets like Bangladesh, Sri Lanka, Myanmar, etc. Even Malaysia's Air Asia has set up ventures in Thailand and India, and is mulling one in Myanmar. Bajaj is an Indian automobile company which has built presence across this group's markets like Indonesia and Sri Lanka for its motor-rickshaws. India's Bharti Airtel has expanded to Bangladesh and Sri Lanka. Apple is the technology leader from the USA that is selling an increasing number of smartphones in Asia, including in the Bay of Bengal markets. As per a Statista.com report on 'Share of Apple's revenue by geographical region', the Asia Pacific (APAC) region comprised ~7.5% of Apple's revenue in the first quarter of 2017 vs. ~5.2% in the fourth quarter of 2015, an over 200 base points (100 base points equals 1%) increase in two years.

In the BRICS story too, the first show of interest had been from companies that were searching for the next-big marketing strategy to focus on, and the large population consumer markets of the BRICS provided that fodder. It helped them make jazzy power-point presentations talking of new markets to target. The asset class story slowly took shape as the consumption buzz spread further, and the foreign trade story is taking proper shape only now, over a decade and a half after the term was coined. In short, businesses went first, then investors followed those businesses, and the trade followed those investors. That was the pecking-order.

In the same way, the large population consumer markets of the Bay of Bengal region can also provide the next-big marketing campaign for businesses. The companies selling consumer products to the Bay of Bengal region have to be shown the scent; the rest will follow in due course. At this juncture, it is worth adding that the average per capita of this group is same as the BRICS a decade ago, and higher than what it was for BRIC back in 2001, when the term itself was coined. The average per capita of the Bay of Bengal region collectively was approximately US$2,100 in 2016, same as that of BRICS in 2006, as per the IMF's WEO data. It is similar even for the BIMSTEC group alone. Moreover, this is double the level where BRICS was back in 2001, i.e. about US$1,000. This number should interest those investors concerned about the relative poverty of these countries. Of course, income level also has to combine with the distribution of income for consumption to be truly widespread, and a later chapter on the Purchasing Power story will further the discussion.

If one looks at the expected CAGR in the per capita income till 2021, then at 8% it is the highest in the Bay of Bengal region. Back in 2001, the CAGR in per capita for the next five years till 2006 had also been the highest in BRICS (along with the East Europe region where Poland, Romania and Czech Republic were picking up).

When talking of a consumption opportunity, statistics may not always be as effective as impressions collected on the ground. For example, Bangladesh is a poorer country than India, per the published statistics. This was the case back in 2005 during my first visit to that country to do a project with Grameen Bank. It was still the case in 2017, during my next visit to that country to make a conference presentation. Back in 2005, the streets of Dhaka had far more luxury sedans than the streets of Indian cities, especially the Nissan, Toyota or Honda luxury sedans. Yes, some of these were second-hand imports from Singapore, but it was a consumption market nonetheless. That would have surprised anyone looking solely at the statistics of per capita income to determine in which country would luxury sedans sell more. This was the case then, paradoxical as it may seem.

And the reason for this was simple. The middle-class segment of the population in Bangladesh was far smaller relative to India in those days. Its people were either business-owners and hence very rich with highly affluent lifestyles, or they were at the bottom of the pyramid. The middle-class, the harbinger of modern consumption stories in many developing countries, was just too small to make a discernible dent on the products seen on the ground. Resultantly, one could see only the luxury sedans driven by the business elite on its streets. The hatch-back budget cars were more commonly seen in Indian streets at that time, typically the first-car purchase in middle-class heavy countries like India. The difference was very catching to the eye! So a car dealer of luxury sedans would have probably maintained better viability than a dealer of hatch-back cars in Dhaka in those days, despite it being a comparatively poorer country. Statistically, Bangladesh was poorer than India, yet the demand for a luxury product was relatively higher there.

Fast forward twelve years from 2005 to 2017, and a lot has changed in Bangladesh. The number of graduates in the country has been increasing each year. Access to higher education has gone up amongst families due to the opening up of more universities. Remittances from family-members in the Gulf nations also helped improve the families' pay for university tuition fees. A number of new corporates have set up shop each year in Dhaka and Chittagong hiring the educated graduates at good salaries. A number of sunrise sectors like healthcare, pharmaceutical, telecom and technology have expanded in the domestic business sector, apart from its traditional garment export sector. Many middle-class neighbourhoods, especially in the northern and the eastern parts of Dhaka city, have seen rapid development due to the demand for housing. All these factors have combined to widen the middle-class base in Dhaka. As a result, hatch-back cars seemed to have increased significantly on its roads now as compared to my previous visit. A car dealer of hatch-back cars would see better viability now in the country than a decade ago. At the same time, Indian cities now sport more luxury sedans because the middle-class population has seen its purchasing power go up over the last decade. In short, statistics alone cannot always convey business-segment specific inferences.

Unfortunately, it is very difficult to quantify this magical middle-class base of countries, especially in the context of products this addressable base may buy. A director of a private equity fund narrowed this to about 200–300 million in India, at an event at the Bombay Management Association. Her estimate was based on certain Census reports. That makes it only 20% of the total population in a large country like India. News articles show that this count is around a similar 20% even in the other large-population countries of the Bay of Bengal group, like Bangladesh and Indonesia. This base has to expand significantly in the coming years, and it is one of the single-biggest commonalities of this region. Of course, one can look at the different sections of per capita income separately to better identify the size of each demographic segment. The intention here was to look at the broader context, to see what works better.

In short, some of these commonalities of this group's countries across the portfolio construct, economic growth construct or equity markets construct might help capture the reader's initial attention, and make them appreciate the relevance of this group's markets.

Moving on to the complementarities

In the mid-2000s, when most of the new BRIC-dedicated portfolio funds were incepted, the main driver of economic growth in most of those countries was exports. The correlation between the growth in exports of goods and the growth in GDP was very high for most of the BRICS countries for the five-years from 2006 to 2011, as per the IMF's WEO data. China had invested a lot into building its manufacturing capacity through most of the 1990s and 2000s; and Brazil, Russia and South Africa (also Australia), exported a lot of the commodities to China to fuel that manufacturing boom. India too showed spurts in investments, exports and consumption, but much of the expectation of the investors in BRICS through the 2000s up until the turn of the decade was built on this commodity export story, especially for Brazil, South Africa and Russia.

But this did not sustain. At the turn of the decade, the Chinese engine slowed from the highs it saw in the previous decades and new waves in global production migration meant some manufacturing left China to find new destinations like Vietnam, Bangladesh and Cambodia. Much of the commodity cycle flowed in a circular fashion between the BRICS countries, so when one member started investing less the others started exporting less, causing stress on the growth of those exporters. Apart from the cyclical factors, a combination of structural defects in the economic composition of Brazil, Russia and South Africa also added to the woes – be it an utter slowdown in investments growth, high external debt, slow pace of reforms, high unemployment, etc. The correlation of their exports growth to GDP growth was unmistakable; and this started coming off as the exports growth slowed. The slowdown in one sector of economic growth was not adequately complemented by the other sectors, and the portfolio as a whole faced downside pressures from the turn of the 2010s.

Similarly, the stories of the Asian countries like South Korea, Malaysia, Thailand and Indonesia also leant towards exports as the primary economic growth driver for most of the 1980s-1990s. These exports needed investments to build that capacity, and so the correlation of the investment growth to the GDP growth in Thailand and Indonesia during the mid-1990s till 1997 was high. These investments were largely funded by external borrowings as their average savings rate was less than the average investments rate in that period. These payments, along with the imports of capital machineries to build those export industries, felt more acute in Thailand whose currency, the Thai Baht, was pegged to the US dollar at that time. When the dollar started rising in the 1990s, Thailand's exports started losing their competitiveness in the global markets and its growth slowed down. This, along with its borrowing repayments, exacerbated the foreign exchange pressure. The Baht had to be freed of the peg, and subsequently the 1997 Asian currency crisis was triggered.

So if one considers a country's national output to be the sum of consumption, investment and net exports, will the economic growth drivers of the countries in the Bay of Bengal group complement each other to protect the group's overall growth trajectory, even if one driver fails? Or is there any overdependence on any one driver like there was in the BRICS in the 2000s or Southeast Asia in the 1990s?

The fair mix of the economic drivers

The fair mix of the economic drivers in the Bay of Bengal group across consumption, investment or net exports is a major complementarity. On exports, its group countries like Bangladesh and Vietnam have notched solid traction in exports growth in the last five years. A lot of production of low-end goods has been migrating from China to Bangladesh and Vietnam, which not only leveraged their advantage of being located close to the shipping trade routes between China to Europe but also made their economies significantly easier places to do business in. In fact, Bangladesh is the only country with a surplus in its current account in South Asia, a region where deficits are more chronic. Bangladesh may see export growth tapering over the next five years, but Vietnam is expected to maintain the momentum. While exports had slowed in Thailand in recent years, they are expected to pick up with a return to political stability. Indonesia is also expected to see some export revival. Even India, pushing its Make in India programme, is expected to see some uptick. Primary commodity and energy exports should also go up from Bhutan and Myanmar as new capacities are added.

On the whole for the Bay of Bengal countries, gross exports formed collectively ~27% of its GDP, as per the data in the CIA World Factbook and the IMF's WEO. This was close to nil in terms of net exports, since these countries also had a high share of gross imports in line with their thrust towards gross investment. In comparison, the share of net export in ASEAN was 5%, 4% in East Europe and 2% in BRICS. Incidentally, this was as high as 5% in the BRICS a decade ago. Between 2006 and 2016, this share has tapered from 5% to 2%. These numbers were a similar 2% and 5% respectively even for the BRICS ex China & India grouping, which indicates the extent of export dependence seen in Brazil, Russia and South Africa a decade ago all of which has tapered since then. Similarly, the journey of Japan, South Korea or Germany through the 1960s to 1980s shows that most of them developed with an export bias while their domestic consumption remained far less.

On investments, Bangladesh, Vietnam, Sri Lanka, Myanmar and Indonesia have all been investing significantly in capacity over the last five years. Imports have also gone up in most of these countries, which coincide to some extent with a growth in their investment rate, indicating that part of the imports were of capital-machinery as part of that investment. That is positive news since it shows the imports were made for productive use, and these assets would realize value in coming years which would help meet the cost of imports to some extent. Investment growth has been sluggish in India from amongst the group's countries and is also expected to decline on an average over the next five years. This is a real worry for a country of its size. On the other hand, investment will either pick up in the other eight group countries or will be held at earlier levels. In all cases, the uptick in investment till 2021 (on CAGR basis) is in line with that of economic growth.

On the whole for the Bengal of Bengal countries (including BIMSTEC alone), gross investment formed ~30% of its GDP, which is a healthy share although slightly less than the 35–40% share seen in rapidly industrializing countries like China in the early 2000s or Malaysia in the 1990s. The MSCI EM Index group clocked an investment rate of 33%, if that serves as a threshold. Even at 30%, the Bay of Bengal group ranks higher than regions like MENA, MINT, NEXT 11, ASEAN, CIVETS, East Africa, Africa (Big Economies), East Europe and Pacific Alliance. In fact, the smaller countries of the group like Myanmar, Bhutan and Nepal had over 40%+ investment rates.

Another point worth noting within the investment scenario is that the share of inventories was between 1–10% in seven out of the nine Bay of Bengal group countries, indicating some ongoing investment is also being done to maintain the stock of capital assets, apart from the initial investment to set up that asset. This is critical to ensure the long-run durability of that machinery or infrastructure.

The example of the Asian currency crisis also showed the ill-effects when investments are funded by external borrowings due to less-than adequate domestic savings. Most of the Bay of Bengal group countries have a high savings rate and a reasonable savings size, which helps meet investments and keeps the deficit challenge within limits. Savings are expected to remain strong in these countries over the next five years. Nepal may see some shortfall in its savings to meet investments, which has picked up disproportionately due to post-earthquake re-building efforts. The main worry is India, where the savings rate has been slipping and is expected to slip further, as consumption becomes over-weight. For those who opine that a country of India's size will be bound to see savings drop as more people enter the consumption-base, China and South Korea can offer good counter examples. China has a larger economic size and consumption-base than India, yet it saves a much higher proportion than India. South Korea also saves a higher proportion than India too, despite being a smaller economic size and consumption-base than India. Yes, gross savings includes not only household savings but also government and corporate savings, nevertheless the broader trend is indicative.

On consumption, India and Thailand have been the leading consumption-driven stories amongst these group countries. Even Bangladesh and Indonesia are expected to see domestic consumption growth over the next five years, which is important given the size of their population. It will also reduce any excess dependence on export for their growth. Further deepening of India's middle-class should also help drive consumption deeper. Even the smaller countries of the group are reasonable consumer bases in themselves. This comprises 60–75% of the GDP in most of the Bay of Bengal group's countries, with Thailand, India and Indonesia bunched around the 70% mark. On the whole for the Bengal of Bengal region, consumption comprises roughly 70% of the collective GDP, quite close to the 65% seen in the MSCI EM Index grouping. Even ASEAN and MENA fall in this range, while NEXT 11, MINT, CIVETS, East Africa, Africa (Big Economies), East Europe, Pacific Alliance notch much higher levels of consumption. Even the SAARC ex India grouping ranks high on consumption because Pakistan, the group's second-largest economy, has a consumption share of over 90%.

Government spending has come off in most of the countries; only India and Myanmar are seeing this pick-up. Hence, private consumption is the main driver of consumption. While inflation in these group countries has not been as high as in some of the bigger emerging markets despite all this consumption, it might need to be brought down further so that the real income of people expands. That is important for consumption.

In short, the drivers of economic growth in this group's countries comprise a fair mix across consumption, investment and export, without a specific bias to any specific driver. Such a fair mix of economic growth drivers should complement each other to maintain the group's overall growth in case any one driver stumbles.

Looking at the correlation of growth-drivers like exports and investments to GDP, the correlation between investment growth and GDP growth for most of the Southeast Asian countries in the 1990s was at the higher end. Even the correlation between export growth and GDP growth in most of the BRICS countries was at the higher end. In the case of the Bay of Bengal group, no one driver has an overtly high correlation for a majority of the countries. In short, the fair mix of the growth-drivers in this group can complement each other for the group's overall growth trajectory.

The major sector exposure

Given that the inherent profile of the BRICS countries was, and remains, oriented around the export of basic commodities; the Materials sector was, and remains, one of the top contributors to the profit pie of the largest 200 listed companies across markets like Brazil, Russia and South Africa. Along with finance and energy, the profit pool in most of the markets of the BRICS continued to have a disproportionate exposure from materials, a commonality that brings a concentration risk to the port-folio apart from the cyclical impact itself. It is no wonder that a slump to the commodity trade hit the investor returns in these markets as badly as it did. Even the profits of the financial and industrial companies who had dealings with these commodity businesses dipped, leading to a domino-impact.

On the other hand, the Bay of Bengal markets offer some variety as far as the major sector exposure of their profit pie is concerned; which can help complement each other even if one sector tanks. Apart from finance and energy, the largest 200 listed companies in Sri Lanka and Vietnam earn a disproportionate share of their profits from the Industrials sector,

Indonesia from Consumer, Bangladesh from Telecom, India from Technology and Thailand from Materials. Given the impact of all these sectors to the overall group's profit pool, it is more diversified without any overt concentration of one sector, especially one which is inherently cyclical. A later chapter on the Sector story discusses this further.

Also, the absolute size of the profits from these markets means that at an overall portfolio-level there is a healthy mix of exposure to manufacturing and services, something similar to South Korea - probably one of the most dynamic emerging markets in recent times. In fact, South Korea was promoted to OECD status as early as 1996, and this combination of its economic profile (along with other factors like infrastructure and growth), might have played a role. If the sector exposure is spread across the economy, it can help minimise the downside risk to the overall portfolio in the event of a slowdown in any one sector, something that the BRICS suffers from.

Opportunities in regional trade

In the Bay of Bengal group, India exports cotton to Bangladesh, which in turn exports readymade garments. Cotton exports to Bangladesh comprise about 40% of India's total cotton exports to the BRICS, Bay of Bengal and South Asian countries, as per the data in Indian Commerce Ministry's commodity-wise export-import data bank. If India can reduce the cost of transport further, or offer more varieties of raw cotton like major cotton-growers like Egypt, it can capture an even larger market share of Bangladesh's cotton imports, a win-win for both countries. Moreover, both legs of the value of the trade are retained with the group itself, which is critical for intra-group trade to grow further.

But does it risk running into a possible cotton cycle crisis, just like the commodity super-cycle afflicted the BRICS? With a significant value migra-tion occurring, and expected, in the garment production value-chain from China to cheaper-labour countries like Bangladesh and Cambodia, the chance of a crash in Bangladesh's garments exports in the near-term seems far less comparatively and ergo, the chance of a crash in India's cotton exports. Not only garment manufacturing, but a number of low-end manufacturing industries are migrating from China to places like Bangladesh and Vietnam due to cheaper costs and easier regulations.

Geographical proximity complements the opportunities for regional value-chains further. The Bay of Bengal group has geographic proximity to each other unlike the BRICS; although time will tell if the group can capitalise on that advantage. If they do, then geographic proximity can complement production migration further. It can use suppliers and ancillary industries from around the region, or the same suppliers from the region that were serving the Chinese market originally, leading to business opportunities for both parties.

Bhutan imports most of its food; and while on a visit to Bhutan's capital Thimphu in 2014, the 'Made in Thailand' food products on the shelves in most department stores was hard to miss. Given the friendly relations and proximity between India and Bhutan, one would have imagined Made in India food products would dominate there. The Made in Thailand labels on the food shelves was too conspicuous. It also highlights that the food trade between Thailand and Bhutan, both part of the Bay of Bengal grouping, is viable despite India being geographically closer. The objective is to show that trade complementarities can exist in this group.

The domestic investors

The Bay of Bengal group is a combination of sizable emerging markets and frontier markets, to use the popular lingo of portfolio investment managers. The portfolio's construct can help by marrying the sheer size of India's markets with the more profitable, less-leveraged and equally high-growth markets of Southeast and South Asia. In short, a portfolio constructed by combining these two can increase the upside from complementary growth drivers while minimizing the downside risks due to diversified sectors and low-correlation. The inherent drivers of most of these economies are not overtly dependent on each other. The degree of correlation between these markets is also less. In fact, a crisis in China or America will probably impact these markets more severely than an internal crisis in any of them or a crisis in a group country – which anyway is a feature almost everywhere today.

Speaking about portfolios, critics can argue why a large market like India needs to be combined with small markets of this group? By being part of a portfolio, India benefits from the better fundamental performance and manufacturing-driven economic models of the group's members, while they benefit from India's scale and services-driven model. India is slipping on key statistics like investment, leverage and savings, while the other group countries fare far better. Thus, this combined portfolio may evince more interest from new funds than a single country fund to India might have done at this point of time. This is more so given the current state of earnings growth in India, which is still waiting to be realized. Any new fund allocating to India may prefer to wait rather than invest so much corpus to India alone at one-go; but a smaller allocation through a group portfolio fund may still be deemed justifiable. That could ensure the aggregate flows continue into India.

In any case, the maturity of domestic financial markets is not a precursor for developing a financial asset class on that region. In fact, being part of a group portfolio becomes a precursor to making the domestic financial market more vibrant by pushing industry and regulators to effect changes, rather than the other way around. India is an example. Back in 2000 when the BRICS story took birth, India's domestic financial markets were still in infancy. It was largely dominated by a few state-run players, with only a handful of private/foreign players setting up shop in a big way. Domestic mutual funds had just started off with the entry of a few private-sector asset managers, as did equity-linked insurance plans. But the BRICS asset class had picked up speed, with the global portfolio funds leading the way with a huge amount of inflows. The inclusion of India into the group only helped hasten the interest towards single-country funds dedicated to India. The portfolio approach gave global funds an initial comfort as it allowed them to take a limited exposure to a new market like India. Once that comfort increased, the case for country funds gained ground. All this pushed the domestic industry further to complement foreign investors. Over time, the domestic asset management companies who had set up shop became big brands in their own right, mobilizing significant assets, customers and volumes. The domestic institutional investor and retail markets deepened, and today they are adequate counterparties to the trades of the global portfolio funds. A decade ago, a sell-off by foreign portfolio investors would have caused the equity markets to fall sharply because there was paucity in the domestic investor space to make up; but now the extent of a potential drop is countered because of adequate domestic investors.

The same story can repeat for the smaller markets in the Bay of Bengal group, as they are in a similar boat now as India was then. A portfolio approach can give investors the initial comfort through a limited exposure, thereafter becoming a basis for larger exposure through country-funds. That would push the case for domestic institutions further, making them adequate counterparties to eventually complement the foreign investors.

This market evolution in India since the 2000s also pushed the case for further financial sector regulations, many of which were not in place in those early years but have been formalized along this journey. It is also pushing more corporate governance changes, which make the system cleaner and more transparent. Recent changes in India have been in areas like annual report disclosures, the composition and accountability of independent directors, etc. Thus, being part of asset class portfolios became the precursor for a more vibrant domestic financial market, complementing the very foreign investors who helped create that grouping.

In conclusion, many investors tend to look more at risks than returns in the post-2008 world; and this might render portfolio acronyms as inevitable rather than passé. If such a portfolio can combine commonalities and complementarities, then perhaps it is cause enough to look at the Bay of Bengal group as a potential asset class. The chapter talked first about the commonalities across the portfolio's construct, economic growth's construct and the equity markets' construct to create the initial awareness of the readers in this group as a whole. Thereafter, it discussed the complementarities in terms of the mix of economic growth-drivers, sector exposure in the profit-pool, trade flows and the push towards domestic investors, which can help push further action. While some of the commonalities and complementarities in these markets are valid today, time will tell the validity of the others.

Did You Know
The Profit Story

During a train journey from Jakarta to Yogyakarta in 2017, an interaction with a fellow passenger was interesting. He worked in Indonesia's financial sector. The conversation went on the Asian currency crisis that had afflicted his market two decades ago, when he had just joined the industry and was plunged straight into chaos. This period had been preceded by a decade of investment and export boom in that country, to the extent that many expatriates opted for a Jakarta posting to get the much-needed Asia work-experience in their bio data. Coincidentally, one such Indian-origin American gentleman was my fellow passenger a couple of days later during a flight to Bali. He had spent several years in the 1980s working in Jakarta during his initial career. Nevertheless, my Indonesian train companion had seen that tide turn, because the 1997 crisis had significant ramifications. Not so much for the country's business environment because that picked up very soon after the crisis stabilized; but more from the perception of Indonesia as a financial market. In fact, this perception extends even to other Southeast Asian markets like Thailand and Malaysia, to some extent.

His economy has come a long way since then, and is now reckoned as one of the leading emerging stories in the ASEAN region. So while global businesses continue to congregate to the Southeast Asian region because all these markets are easy places to do business in, their regulations are reasonable, consumer sentiment is high and spending capacity of the people remains robust; the global investors still do not come to the extent they should. These markets merit far higher investor interest than they do currently. Indonesia itself has a well-developed financial market. In fact, the total market capitalisation of the stock exchange in Jakarta is similar to those in Bangkok and Kuala Lumpur, despite those economies being relatively more developed. The stock exchange building in Jakarta's business district looks as dapper as the iconic PJ Towers which houses the Bombay stock exchange in India. Of course, the look of a building is not indicative of its potential as an investment destination; nevertheless investor interest still remains far less than what it should be.

The gentleman added an interesting titbit here, something that caused him both cheer and sorrow. The Philippines is Indonesia's often-compared peer amongst ASEAN emerging economies. In 2016, Indonesia's stock market saw a higher number of listed large companies delivering YoY profit growth over 2015 as compared to the Philippines. Not many are aware of this fact. In the backdrop of the inevitable comparisons that occur between Indonesia and the Philippines as the next powerhouses of Southeast Asia, this was a cause of cheer for him in front of the analysts/investors who compare their markets. This is also a sorrow for him because it reminds him of the sheer under-awareness his market still suffers in the eyes of the global investor community, who he thinks make more buzz about his peers on the other side of the South China Sea.

Why is the buzz louder about the Philippines? His view was perhaps it was the result of the Asian currency crisis that still makes investors sceptical to take a closer look at Indonesia, one of the four main afflicted markets at that time. Perhaps it is the colonial-era history that the Philippines shares with the USA that fuelled better awareness about that country, at least amongst the larger American investors. Perhaps it is the language barrier of the local industry-people. Bahasa Indonesia is still the main tongue of communication, even in most offices of the educated white-collars. That can create a challenge for foreigners to navigate the local markets. On the other hand, most Filipinos are proficient in English. Reasons can be several; and it does highlight a plague of under-awareness and under-appreciation that many markets of this region still suffer from, despite them now becoming noteworthy in their own right.

This situation is more tragic given that the next generation of Indonesians seemed enterprising enough. For instance, the business students in my guest-lectures in Jakarta gave relevant answers to my situational business case study questions; something I had found even in Bangladesh. As this next generation enters the job front, continuity of this investor under-appreciation might be counter-productive from the perspective of creating a motivating ecosystem for local corporates to innovate and grow. Vibrant financial markets form an integral part of creating a motivating ecosystem for local start-ups and corporates, India being a prime example. It is imperative that the global investor community increases its appreciation of these markets that are churning out good results relative to their more-hyped counterparts. Hence the chapter's title – Did You Know!

Bloomberg data of the largest 200 listed companies by 2016 market capitalisation has some interesting findings for this group's markets. This study includes the largest 200 companies from each of these following seventeen markets - large emerging markets like China, Russia, Brazil, South Africa, South Korea, Mexico, Turkey, Nigeria, Thailand and India as well as new emerging stories like Pakistan, Saudi Arabia, Indonesia, Vietnam, Bangladesh, Sri Lanka and the Philippines. All in all, this sample set had about 3,200 companies under study.

Consistency in ROE

How many companies from this sample delivered a 10% plus ROE annually in each of the five preceding years, using ROE as the base method of comparing consistency in corporate performance? Of the 3,200 companies across the sample, only 940 had delivered a 10% ROE in each of the last five years. Of these 940 companies, 43% were from the Bay of Bengal group, while only one-third were from the BRICS, 25% were from ASEAN, 30% from SAARC and 20% from MINT. Each of the six Bay of Bengal markets had over 50 companies that delivered 10% plus ROE consecutively in each of the preceding five years. Only Pakistan, China, Turkey and South Africa from the others crossed this threshold while South Korea, Mexico, Russia and Nigeria (all considered as major emerging markets) each notched only about half of this percentage. Looking at Indonesia and the Philippines specifically, Indonesia had 66 companies crossing this mark vs. 46 in the Philippines.

Improvement in ROE

While the level of average ROE of the largest 200 companies across each of these seventeen markets slipped between the last five-years from 2016 and 2012, the only notable exception, Vietnam, is part of the Bay of Bengal group. Within the Bay of Bengal markets itself, the decline in the level of average ROE over these five preceding years has been less in Thailand, Vietnam, Sri Lanka and Bangladesh than in India, a point in their favour. All the six Bay of Bengal markets maintained double-digit average ROEs in 2016. Bangladesh, Indonesia, Thailand and Sri Lanka all notched ~13–14%, with only China, Pakistan and South Africa ahead of them. India and Vietnam followed with 10–11%. The ROE and profit margins for the Bay of Bengal group collectively were higher than the BRICS ex China grouping in 2016. In any case, the range between the ROEs earned by the constituent markets at either extreme was as high as 600 base points in the BRICS vs. only 200 base points in the Bay of Bengal group. From the perspective of investing in such a group portfolio, one would desire a lower range since it implies the profit growth is better synchronised across the markets of the group.

The five-year CAGR in aggregate profits across each of these markets between 2012 and 2016 was reasonably positive in only nine of these seventeen markets, showing the stress in the broader universe. Within the six Bay of Bengal markets in this sample, four registered a positive growth in profits. The five-year CAGR in the average profit per company was -5% in India, -14% in Russia, -21% in Brazil, -5% in South Africa, -5% in Mexico, -4% in Indonesia, -2% in Turkey and -2% in Saudi Arabia. Conversely, this was 9% in China, 9% in Pakistan, 8% in the Philippines, 5% in Vietnam, 5% in Thailand, 3% in Sri Lanka, 2% in Bangladesh and 2% in South Korea. The five-year CAGR taken collectively for the group was better in the Bay of Bengal than the BRICS ex China grouping, SAARC, MINT, Pacific Alliance and Africa (Big Economies); BRICS ex China is used here because the far better profit numbers of Chinese companies pulls up the average for the BRICS.

Within the Bay of Bengal markets, Vietnam, Thailand, Sri Lanka and Bangladesh had a positive bias while India and Indonesia were the laggards. Indonesia's case is explained to some extent by the large exceptional losses in a couple of its companies, Astra and Borneo Lumbung. The

redeeming aspect for the group is that they have a wider base of companies achieving profitability, despite a few exceptional cases pulling down
the market's average. A wider base creates more individual investible
opportunities to look at in this group.

ROE components as per the Du-Pont formula

The Du-Pont formula breaks up ROE into profit margins, productivity and
leverage. On profit margins, Thailand and Vietnam, part of the Bay of
Bengal group, showed the highest improvement in the level of profit
margin between 2016 and 2012, along with Pakistan. All the remaining
markets in the sample saw a slippage in their overall profit margins earned
between 2016 and 2012, or they saw it remain flat. Within the Bay of
Bengal markets itself, this dip was far less in Bangladesh and Sri Lanka than
in India while Indonesia was similar to India, a point in their favour. The
average five-year profit margin earned by the largest 200 companies in
each of the sample markets between 2012 and 2016 was the highest in
China and Saudi Arabia at 13% plus, with Brazil, Mexico, South Korea and
Vietnam at the other end of the spectrum at 4–6%. The remaining
markets, including the rest of the Bay of Bengal ones, notched average
margins between these ranges.

In terms of the count of profitable companies in the year 2016, Vietnam,
Bangladesh, Thailand, Indonesia, India and Sri Lanka notched up the highest
numbers along with South Korea and China. They remain ahead of larger
emerging market peers like Mexico, Pakistan, Turkey, Saudi Arabia,
Nigeria, Brazil and Russia and the Philippines. About 2800 companies from
this sample delivered a profit in 2016. Back in 2012, about 200 companies
out of these 2800 had shown a loss, thus implying these 200 companies
improved their profitability to deliver a profit five years later. Out of this
200, about one-fourth came from the Bay of Bengal markets.

The percentage of companies from each market which delivered positive
growth in profits in terms of five-year CAGR between 2012 and 2016
was the highest in China, Pakistan, Bangladesh, Sri Lanka and India (over
50% in each), followed by Thailand, Vietnam, Indonesia, South Korea and
the Philippines (over 40% in each). All the six markets of the Bay of Bengal
group feature here. The percentages in the other large emerging markets,

including those of the BRICS, were almost half of these. This can be termed as the breadth of the profit makers in the market, although stock exchanges use the term breadth to refer to the price movement of the companies. A higher number indicates a wider-base of profit growth, reducing the concentration risk of profit makers. For the Bay of Bengal group as a whole, this ratio was 43%, far higher than the 30% in the BRICS and SAARC each, 26% in ASEAN and 16% in BRICS ex China. This indicates the extent of bleeding in the larger markets.

In short, profitable stories abound in this group, if that is a reason enough to evince investor interest. From the 3,200 companies in the sample, about 280 companies saw a 30% plus CAGR in profits over the last five-years from 2012 to 2016. Over 40% of these 280 companies were from the Bay of Bengal markets. In comparison, only 25% were from the BRICS. The larger emerging markets like South Korea, Mexico, Turkey, Nigeria and the Philippines also comprised only about 25% each. Of the 850-odd companies that saw a 10% plus CAGR in profits over the last five years, over 40% came from the Bay of Bengal markets. Of the 140 companies that saw a CAGR of 50% plus in profits over the last five years, again 40% of them were from the Bay of Bengal markets.

On productivity, there was an across-the-board drop in the average productivity between the five-years from 2012 to 2016 in all the sample markets. This has probably been the biggest contributor towards the dip in average ROEs across this period. Sweating of assets across the emerging market universe remains inadequate, partly due to systemic challenges of a sluggish global economy and over-capacity and partly due to each individual market's inefficiencies. However, this drop in productivity was amongst the lowest in Bangladesh and Vietnam, a point in their favour. Most large emerging markets fared worse. The average five-year productivity for the largest 200 companies in the sample markets between 2012 and 2016 was the highest in Thailand, Sri Lanka, Vietnam, South Korea, Russia, Pakistan and Mexico, followed by India, Indonesia, Turkey, Brazil, South Africa and the Philippines. The average five-year productivity for the Bay of Bengal group collectively was amongst the highest relative to the other peer regions, along with BIMSTEC, ASEAN, MINT, BRICS ex China and Pacific Alliance. The MSCI EM Index grouping as a whole had an average productivity lower than the above-mentioned groups during this period.

On leverage, Thailand, Indonesia and Vietnam saw a reduction in their leverage levels between 2012 and 2016 despite their average leverage remaining less than most of their peers, indicating the potential headroom for further growth by taking on more debt capital. Conversely, leverage has gone up appreciably between 2012 and 2016 in markets like Bangladesh, Turkey, Brazil, Russia and the Philippines, constraining their headroom for growth. BRICS markets like Brazil, Russia and India face a double-whammy, with increasing leverage on one end and declining ROEs on the other. For the Bay of Bengal group collectively, the average leverage ratio has remained largely stable between 2012 and 2016, while it has risen in the BRICS and Pacific Alliance. The average five-year leverage in the sample markets between 2012 and 2016 was the highest in Nigeria, Turkey, China and Bangladesh, followed by India, Vietnam, Pakistan, Brazil and South Africa. At the same time, it was amongst the least in the Bay of Bengal markets like Thailand, Sri Lanka and Indonesia. The average five-year leverage for the Bay of Bengal group collectively was less than the BRICS, MENA, SAARC and Africa (Big Economies). The MSCI EM Index grouping also had higher leverage than the Bay of Bengal group during this period.

Operating leverage seems to be kicking in across markets like Pakistan, Vietnam and Nigeria, as their last five-year profit growth from 2012 to 2016 exceeded their revenue growth. One of these is part of the Bay of Bengal group. Operating leverage is yet to kick in across markets like Bangladesh, India, Sri Lanka, Indonesia, South Korea, China, Mexico, Saudi Arabia and the Philippines, as their profit growth lagged the positive growth they clocked in their revenue. Four of these are part of the Bay of Bengal group. Cost-control seems to be the vogue in markets like Thailand that maintained profit growth in this period despite a dip in revenue growth. At the other end, markets like Brazil, Russia, South Africa and Turkey struggle with both declining revenue and profit growth, each worse than the other. At the same time, all the six Bay of Bengal markets along with others like South Korea, China, Mexico, Saudi Arabia and the Philippines clocked a higher growth rate in their equity capital as compared to their growth in profits during this five-year period, possibly indicating some fresh investment is made into expanding the operations and capacity of the business.

India's challenge

India's economic story is yet to translate into a corporate story, and except for a few multi-baggers, many promising equity stocks are yet to deliver on profits. From India's context given its current state of profitability, it may be to its advantage to combine in a group portfolio with the South and Southeast Asian markets which are delivering relatively better fundamental performance. The aggregate basket may look more favourable from the risk-return perspective than just the individual market or even the existing baskets it is part of. It is currently part of several Asia ex Japan and the emerging market portfolios, but the larger emerging markets have severely lagged in profitability and ROE, resulting in outflows from some funds in recent years. On the other hand, combining with more vibrant performers in a Bay of Bengal portfolio might be a more favourable basket for India to be part of in the current context. The Southeast and South Asian markets add better margins and lower leverage into the equation, while India brings the scale. After all, both factors play a role in investing mandates of global portfolio investors. Such a combination may help evince further investor interest and channel more inflows than what they might have been otherwise. Yes, it is true that funds have separate investment mandates to look at emerging markets and frontier markets and so their monies cannot be mixed, but asset managers can start new funds dedicated to these better-off markets from the fresh monies they receive. That itself is one of the objectives of the portfolio asset class idea.

In any case, the universe of under-performers still has far more investor interest than it merits. Most of the constituents of BRICS have underperformed, yet the number of funds which have a high allocation to these markets is still more than those to the better-performing markets. For instance, more than 12,000 portfolio funds globally had over 10% allocation to Brazil, as of February 2017 according to Bloomberg's data. Similarly, South Africa had 1,100, Mexico had 1,000, Turkey had 700 and Russia had 660. In comparison, Thailand had only 400, Indonesia had only 380, Vietnam had 80, Bangladesh had 18 and Sri Lanka had 11. Some of these funds are sticking their monies to the BRICS markets on the hopes of a revival, but the issue is that Brazil, Russia and South Africa have been plagued by both cyclical headwinds and structural shortcomings. A reversal in oil and commodity prices from their lows of recent years may address the cyclical issue, but the structural challenges like an overdependence on oil and commodity export earnings, high debt and fiscal pressures still remain. Unless the structural issues are fixed, investor interest will be dependent on short-term swings.

Whether this combination of sizable and profitable stories is a reason good enough to evince investor interest in a portfolio on the Bay of Bengal markets can be debated, but it does take the discussion back to the gentleman in the Indonesian train. The investing public is under-aware and under-appreciative of certain markets which perhaps merit better attention. How many were aware of the profit performance comparisons mentioned in this chapter? If money chases performance, the reality should have been otherwise. However, that presupposes the bridge was built for the money to cross. This book is just an attempt to build that bridge.

Even the best indicator of investor appreciation (or excitement) of any market – valuation is still relatively lower in these markets, despite delivering relatively better results. Of course, it is always tough to say what the threshold valuation acceptable for a market is because it depends on a number of factors. The historical price to earnings ratio is amongst the lowest in the Bay of Bengal markets. Vietnam and Sri Lanka had one of the lowest average PE ratios within this sample, based on the 2016 historical earnings. This is similar to the levels seen in South Korea, China and Nigeria. Bangladesh and Thailand had an average PE ratio similar to Mexico, South Africa and the Philippines. India is an outlier, and it is comparable to Brazil and Mexico. These valuations are not based on forward earnings and so are incomplete, but may still offer some relative comparison.

The challenge of size

The main challenge of the Bay of Bengal group markets is size. Despite their better relative standing on metrics like ROE, profit margins, financial and operating leverage, they are smaller in size than most of the large emerging markets, which reduces the comfort of global portfolio investors from the liquidity perspective. Looking at the profit per company as a yardstick of the average size of the companies in these markets, then China, South Korea, Russia and India, in that order, formed the largest four in this sample of seventeen in 2016.

But at the same time, the Bay of Bengal group's markets are also not as small as imagined to be. For example, Thailand and Indonesia are similar in size to the larger emerging markets like Turkey, Mexico and Saudi Arabia, while Bangladesh is similar in size to Nigeria. The average profit per company of the Bay of Bengal group collectively (including that of BIMSTEC) is similar in size to peer regions like MINT, GCC, SAARC and Pacific Alliance, and is actually larger than ASEAN, MENA and Africa (Big Economies). Hence, if an investor is comfortable with the average size of companies in these regions, then the Bay of Bengal should also merit a look. At the same time, the growth in the average profit size between 2012 and 2016 has been the highest in Bay of Bengal group markets like Bangladesh and Vietnam, from amongst this sample, followed by China and Pakistan. Conversely, all the BRICS ex China markets along with Mexico and Turkey saw some of the sharpest dips.

On an average market capitalisation basis, the average size of a company in Thailand or Indonesia is similar to Russia, South Africa or Saudi Arabia, while Bangladesh is similar to Nigeria. Of course, the view of size and liquidity extends to the metric of trading volumes of that market, and that is discussed in a later chapter.

The challenge of capacity

The other predicament is the possibility of over-capacity in the economic system. Global GDP growth has been only 0.6% CAGR since the five-years from 2012 to 2016, which has rendered global demand sluggish. At the same time, competition has intensified further. Thirty years ago, competition for the developing markets was mainly amongst US, European and Japanese companies. Then companies from South Korea, Japan and Taiwan followed. Now, even companies from a plethora of developing countries have joined in this bandwagon. They have become leading brands in their own right. This competitive intensity, along with subdued global demand, has created an over-supply of companies all fighting for the same demand pool. So while the number of companies increased, their profitability has not increased commensurately.

Profits earned by a company becomes a yardstick for their next year's budgets; which gives an indication of the investments it is making into critical expansion of plants, talent and resources. If a company is not increasing its profit pool, then its ability to expand its budget in those areas of future growth becomes curtailed. This is a double-whammy in the long-run, since not only is it not making money now, but its ability to make money in future is also hit. So the small remain small, and struggle to grow.

Nevertheless, one advantage in a scenario of sluggish global demand is that domestic consumption is a saving grace. The earlier chapter on Asset Class share some data on the consumption base of the Bay of Bengal group markets. Consumption was often frowned upon as unnecessary in the socialist-era India of the 1960s and 1970s. Now with the sizable domestic consumer base in group countries like Bangladesh, Indonesia, Thailand, India, Vietnam and even Sri Lanka, the pain of the global slow-down is cushioned to an extent, an investment rationale in itself.

In conclusion, this chapter has looked at several data of ROE, profits, margins, productivity and leverage to demonstrate that the Bay of Bengal group markets have delivered good fundamental performance relative to its more-hyped peers between 2012 and 2016. It has looked at the consistency and improvement in these metrics, how the components of ROE compare, as well as certain challenges these markets face. Nevertheless, a long road is still left to lift the level of awareness and appreciation of these markets on the lines of the larger emerging markets. An asset class may help further that objective by setting up of dedicated portfolios that want to be part of these markets' journey.

Adding a post-script on the increasing divergence between corporate stories in many emerging markets, as much as 20% of the companies from the ten largest emerging markets in this sample that were profitable back in 2012 became unprofitable in 2016. The varying nature of profitability makes a clear case for active investment strategy now more than ever. It is more important to identify individual bottom-up stories for long term winners, rather than going only by the benchmark indices to invest in emerging and frontier markets. Indices do not evince much investor confidence in the current context. A portfolio built on an active strategy may yield better results from these markets in the long term. Hence, the need to build awareness and appreciation of these individual markets becomes all the more acute.

Stock, Flow and Spread
The Purchasing Power Story

During 2014, whilst on a quick trip to Delhi to catch up with a friend who had a transit before returning to Pakistan, her opinion about a certain statistic of her country was interesting to hear. This was on the habit of savings. As per her opinion, most Pakistanis seem to emphasise the quality of current lifestyle, which typically means the habit of spending far outstrips the habit of saving. They do not want to compromise on current lifestyle, and would rather compromise on current saving just to experience instant consumption. Most people there often start thinking of saving when they have an adequate surplus to do so, even if it means after the age crosses 30 or 40. Most families, given the type of social structures still existing in many households, seem to depend on children for providing for their future.

Her observation may only be opinion, but Pakistan's statistics reaffirm this. The IMF'S WEO data shows that Pakistan has had a gross savings rate to GDP ratio of as low as 13–14% since the 1980s; and it has rarely crossed ~16%. The highest it has notched in recent history was 20% in 2002–2003, after which it again turned south. These are abnormally low numbers as compared to its peers in the South Asian region. Bangladesh has seen its savings rate move from ~25% to ~30% during this period. India's touched a high of ~35% before dipping to the late-20s. Sri Lanka, which saw rates range from ~25% to ~30%, is expected to cross the ~30% mark over the next five years. Even Southeast Asian nations like Thailand, Indonesia and Vietnam have ranged from the late-20s to early-30s. It is perhaps for good reason that the Bay of Bengal group (or even the BIMSTEC) does not include Pakistan, an economy which is high-growth and profitable yet invests and saves far less than it should.

A more appropriate example for Pakistan may be China, its closest geopolitical ally. China enjoys a gross savings rate of over ~40%, even touching ~50% in recent years. Of course, gross savings of a country includes the savings across households, corporations and government, not just the household; but its household saving rate could not be divergently less than this even after accounting for the high profitability its companies have made. In fact, China's numbers rejects the claims that many governments often make to defend the declining rates of savings in their countries – that a higher level of spending is needed to sustain a high rate of growth.

Amongst the major emerging markets, only Nigeria, Brazil and South Africa rank as low as Pakistan, followed by Turkey. The good news is that Pakistan's savings rate is expected to rise to 16–17% over the next five years, as per the IMF's WEO data projections. That is a solid 300 base points increase; the only hitch being that even 16–17% is still severely lower than what a country in Pakistan's stage of economic development needs. The savings crisis has only exacerbated the extent of external borrowings its government has had to take up in recent years to fund investment projects; and the recent pressures on its currency, the Pakistani Rupee, reflect that.

The data on savings is very robust in the Southeast Asian countries. It is not that consumerism is any less there. Most urban metro-train stations in their cities are connected through shopping malls, clearly pushing the marketing strategy of impulse-buying. Every other commercial establishment is a shopping mall, and most of them are of a scale far larger than the malls in India. Yet they save as much. Upon asking the locals in the universities in those countries, their view was that it was a combination of factors – their memory of the 1990s crisis that left them suddenly poor, the increasing nuclear family culture which means one cannot depend solely on children and/or the marketing campaigns of products by the banks. This has pushed a culture of savings in the Southeast Asian region since the last two decades; and so despite the great consumerism push, people are balancing their saving and spending habits. This is yet to take off in markets like Pakistan.

In simple definition, the habit of saving is simply the ability or inability to give up something today for getting something better tomorrow. Opinions of both sides, to save now or spend now, are well grounded.

After all, the very point of earning is to spend it and have a good life, if one looks at the consumer's perspective. Current consumption is a significant driver of economic growth. From the economy's perspective, if everyone saves and does not spend, then economic growth may taper down. After all, consumer demand creates a whole chain of economic activity, which survives on the spending habit of the citizenry. That approach is good as long as some portion of a person's needs for tomorrow is taken care of. So the real crux is to balance spending and savings so that current consumption does not come at the cost of future consumption. The question that precedes this is why is savings needed in the first place? Is it really necessary to save?

Why are savings (stock) important?

The extent of savings (or stock of wealth) impacts the purchasing power of the citizens, which in turn impacts which businesses ultimately have long term opportunity in that growing economy. This can be the future purchasing power, as well as current purchasing power in certain cases. The stock of saving is critical because it ensures the continued consumption of people even during periods of unemployment, when current income faces a drag. The stock of saving is critical because it ensures the continued consumption of people even after they stop working and retire. The stock of saving is critical because it ensures the consumption of people where large upfront payments have to be furnished. More examples galore!

The income of these markets has to be looked at both as a flow and stock concept. If the flow is the current income a person earns every year, then stock is the savings block which sustains his or her propensity to consume in the future years or for items that need a larger outlay. As economies evolve and their consumer buying habits evolve, many products end up being bought by both the flow and the stock of income, not just the flow alone.

In many developing countries, while citizens have a growing wallet today because they are concurrently earning, their wallet may not remain large in future once they stop earning. Their future purchasing power may be hit, which may impact business and investor interest. The rapid economic growth in developing countries might make them compelling consumption markets today, but businesses need to invest in the long term if they are to make significant money. Fund managers looking at such markets strategically also want to invest for the long term, which presupposes its businesses have a long term story in the first place. If its story has an expiry date, it may not look attractive as a long term strategy, but only as a short-term tactical allocation. That means hot money flows, something not desirous for the overall stability of financial markets.

Just because an economy is growing fast, it does not mean there is an opportunity for every type of business. The composition of its purchasing power might not provide adequate commercial sense for too many players to enter that market. Pakistan itself has been a high-growth economy in recent years, despite all the concerns over its recent political challenges. Does this translate into ample opportunity for all sorts of businesses? No! If Pakistani citizens do not have adequate savings (stock), their spending abilities will primarily depend on the size of their current income (flow). Another example is South Africa, which has high income-concentration, low savings rate and high unemployment. Imagine the debilitating impact of this toxic mixture on the sustained flow of consumption in that economy. The broader-base of consumers is out of the market for most discretionary products during phases of unemployment. The situation may not be so severe in Pakistan since it has comparatively less income concentration and unemployment, despite not faring well on savings rate.

Another reason why savings are important is because it hastens the development of the domestic financial sector into becoming adequate counterparties to foreign investors. For instance, savers typically migrate from consumption to investment as they reach a higher savings threshold; at which point they start saving in investment products. Not just bank deposits, but even domestic mutual funds and insurance funds get a lift-up as demand drives the push to establishing this segment. This eventually makes the domestic investor market large enough as counterparties to foreign fund managers, who would eventually look to exit their holdings.

A product example can better explain the impact on current consumption, not including future consumption. Housing finance is a core need in high-growth developing countries that are seeing societal changes like nuclearisation and urbanisation; which in turn is driving residential mortgage demand. Since a home loan has an initial lump sum down-payment (owner's equity), it necessitates the person having an adequate stock of wealth to be able to pay such a lump sum. This is apart from the flow of income one needs to show as credit worthiness, in order to make the regular repayment instalments. Of course, one can always borrow a short-term personal loan to furnish that lump sum own equity, but that new debt would only distort their credit worthiness for the housing finance company. Alternatively, he or she can borrow this lump sum amount from friends and family, but this only makes the borrower further financially dependent.

In short, a person may earn a current income of millions of rupees in Pakistan, but if he does not have adequate savings to meet the down-payment portion of the mortgage, how can any housing finance company extend a loan to him? Any housing finance company would feel constrained by this limitation of the market opportunity, despite the good economic growth rates of Pakistan. Unless the market opportunity expands, the prospects to deepen the business will be constrained due to the narrow addressable consumer base; thus restricting the aggregate number of players who see commercial sense to enter that market.

Home loan is a very important segment in any high-growth economy, since it has a multiplier impact on other industries like cement, plastics, steel, rubber, etc. Imagine the loss of potential opportunity these ancillary sectors face in the long term. With a savings rate of only 16–17% expected in Pakistan over the next few years, the fundamental opportunity of this market is curtailed, irrespective of any noise by its industry participants. Housing finance is just one example. There are other industries as well that depend on savings.

Typically, as nations mature and average income increases, the propensity to spend on discretionary items goes up. There is a simple explanation for this – the growing disposable surplus offers more room to spend on items bought at one's discretion (or choice). It is worth adding that the very use of the word discretionary is ironical, given that most consumers eventually feel compelled or addicted to go on buying the products that were deemed discretionary. Many lifestyle products fall under this; things one cannot just do without after using it for some time. Cigarettes are a common example, as is buying the latest i-phone variant. They were bought on discretion once, but the habit of it makes one a compulsive spender for it irrespective of income flows.

What alternative is there then but to turn to one's savings block? Over a period of time, many discretionary items may end up being bought from saving, not solely from the flow of income. If the citizenry had maintained reasonable savings, they can go on buying such items without a major hitch and those businesses can sustain their market opportunity for a longer period. If the citizens have inadequate savings, they might limit buying which constraints the market opportunity or perhaps creates new social evils to be able to go on buying (for instance, buying alcohol by forgoing the family's budget for food grains).

Comparing expected savings

Coming back to the perspective of purchasing power, the question to ask at this juncture is — are developing countries saving enough? Are they expected to go on saving enough? Will their growth translate into a substantial boost to their purchasing power of tomorrow?

Using the IMF'S WEO data, the expected gross savings rate by 2021 for the Bay of Bengal group collectively is expected to be 30%. The same holds for BIMSTEC. Only BRICS, ASEAN and the GCC enjoy a savings rate higher than 30%. It is followed by NEXT 11 and MENA at 28% each, SAARC (27%), CIVETS (26%), MINT (25%), East Europe (24%) and Pacific Alliance (22%), while East Africa and Africa (Big Economies) are expected to see savings rates less than 20%. The MSCI EM Index as a whole is expected to have a savings rate of 26%, if that serves as a benchmark.

The expected CAGR in GDP over the next five years till 2021 is expected to be the highest in the Bay of Bengal group at 9% (including for BIMSTEC alone), along with SAARC and East Africa. It is followed by the BRICS and ASEAN at 8% each, and then followed by Africa (Big Economies), MINT, East Europe, CIVETS and NEXT 11 at 7% each, Pacific Alliance and MENA at 6% each and GCC at 5%. The MSCI EM Index grouping is expected to grow its combined GDP at a 7% CAGR.

The absolute size of the savings pie expected in 2021 indicates the quantum of the purchasing power opportunity. A market may be a high savings one, but if it is miniscule in size, that does not augur well for business potential either. The gross savings size expected by 2021 is the highest in BRICS (US$9.1 billion), followed by the NEXT 11 (US$2.5 billion), Bay of Bengal (US$1.9 billion), BRICS ex China (US$1.9 billion), MENA (US$1.4 billion), BIMSTEC (US$1.3 billion), SAARC (US$1.2 billion), MINT (US$1.2 billion), ASEAN (US$1.1 billion), CIVETS (US$1.1 billion), East Europe (US$0.9 billion), BRICS ex China & India (US$0.9 billion), GCC (US$0.5 billion), Pacific Alliance (US$0.5 billion), Africa (Big Economies) (US$0.3 billion) and East Africa (US$0.1 billion). Figures for BRICS ex China are shown here to remove the disproportional impact of a large market like China. It is worth noting that the Bay of Bengal group is of a similar savings size as the BRICS ex China grouping. This is expected to be $5.2 billion for the MSCI EM Index grouping. The median savings rate is about 26.7% for these groups, the median GDP growth is about 7.2% and the median savings size is $1 billion.

Now if all these three metrics – savings rate, GDP growth and savings size expected over the coming years are put into a single graph, then only four groups fall within the category of high savings rate plus high economic growth plus reasonable savings size. This is the veritable sweet-spot from the perspective of the stock position. These four groups include the BRICS, ASEAN, Bay of Bengal (including BIMSTEC) and SAARC. Due to the inclusion of high-growth markets like India and Bangladesh, BIMSTEC will also enjoy a better growth rate than ASEAN or BRICS. Groups like NEXT 11, GCC and MENA also have a high savings rate and size, but they fall behind in economic growth. Similarly, East Africa has high growth, but a low savings rate and savings size. At the other end, groups like MINT, CIVETS, Pacific Alliance, East Europe and Africa (Big Economies) lag in both savings rate and economic growth, despite notching decent savings size.

The comparison is more interesting if one looks at the "ex" regions. Those comparing BIMSTEC with SAARC, the South Asian group, may note that BIMSTEC will have a higher savings rate and a marginally larger savings size, despite their expected economic growth rates being similar. BRICS ex China ranks way low on savings rate while BRICS ex China & India slips even further, which coincides with the lower level of savings in Brazil, Russia and South Africa. Even their expected economic growth is lower, which coincides with the near-term growth outlook of these three constituent markets of BRICS. Even SAARC ex India slips on savings rate as its second-largest economy, Pakistan, struggles with a low savings rate. The weight of Pakistan in the SAARC pulls back its average, while Thailand, Bangladesh, etc. push up BIMSTEC's average. In fact, BIMSTEC ex India also sees good economic growth and a high savings rate. This might provide ample counter-argument to those critics who feel that the Bay of Bengal group's story is of India's alone, and the other markets are of low consequence.

Comparing this data with where the BRICS markets stood a decade ago also provides interesting insights on how the large emerging markets view savings. Back in 2006, the BRICS grouping had a similar savings rate as they are expected to have in 2021; and the same holds true for the BRICS ex China and BRICS ex China & India groupings. This indicates that the savings culture has remained firm in these large markets, despite the rolling of the years in interim. On the other hand, the Bay of Bengal group has seen a slight dip in its savings rate from a decade ago in 2006, as compared to the level it is expected to reach by 2021. Since the decadal savings rate in the case of BIMSTEC ex India grouping has remained largely firm, it reaffirms the impact of the slippage in India's savings rate over the coming years, while Russia, Brazil, South Africa or China are not expected to see such a dip in their savings rate despite recent economic performances. India's savings rate has been declining in recent years from its earlier highs, following the consumption-driven frenzy that has picked up in the country. Comparatively, the other players in the group are able to maintain their savings rate, or at least see a lesser dip. India may have seen household financial savings pick up in recent years, especially after the November 2016 demonetisation and regulatory changes in the real estate sector with the Real Estate Regulation and Development Act (RERA Act) in 2016, which rendered real estate investments relatively less attractive, leading to a migration of real estate investments to financial savings. Nevertheless, it is imperative that India picks up its overall savings rate even further, so that its long term savings stock can benefit.

At this juncture, let us turn to the individual countries and see how they rank on their expected savings rate, economic growth and savings size by 2021. Most of the BIMSTEC countries like India, Thailand, Bangladesh, Nepal, Sri Lanka, Myanmar, as well as the extended Bay of Bengal group markets like Indonesia and Vietnam, all fall in, or around, the veritable sweet-spot.

Expected savings rate is close to ~30% or higher in markets like China, Iran, South Korea, Nepal, Bhutan, Indonesia, Ethiopia, Sri Lanka, Bangladesh, Thailand and Saudi Arabia. Vietnam and India follow closely. Most of the Bay of Bengal markets are included here. At the other end, the savings rate is expected to be amongst the lowest in markets like Brazil, South Africa, Poland, Myanmar, Pakistan, Nigeria, Ghana and Kenya. The average five-year savings rate from now till 2021 is also expected to include the above-mentioned markets, which shows the trajectory is consistent. The only hitch is that most of the Bay of Bengal markets, including India, Thailand, Bangladesh and Vietnam, are expected to see a slight dip in their savings rate in 2021 vs. 2016. Expected economic CAGR will be between 8–10% in India, Bangladesh, Indonesia, Vietnam, Ethiopia, Malaysia, Kenya, Tanzania, Romania, Nepal, Myanmar, Cambodia and the Philippines, followed by 6–7% in Thailand, Sri Lanka, Brazil, Mexico, Poland, Russia, Colombia, Peru and Pakistan, with South Korea, Turkey, Egypt, Saudi Arabia and Chile following below 5%. Expected savings rate is the highest in India, China, South Korea, Russia, Brazil, Indonesia, Thailand, Mexico, Malaysia, Vietnam, Turkey, Saudi Arabia and the Philippines. India has a high absolute savings size second only to China amongst developing countries. Indonesia's savings size is as large as major emerging markets like South Korea, Russia or Brazil. In the same manner, the savings size of Bangladesh, Thailand and Vietnam are as large as Malaysia, Nigeria, Poland or the UAE and even larger than Egypt, Pakistan, Chile or South Africa. Nepal, Sri Lanka and Myanmar have a smaller savings size in line with their economic weight, although these are still larger than the East African lions of Kenya or Tanzania.

Based on this, only eight out of the thirty-odd countries in this experiment fall in the category of high savings rate, high economic growth and reasonable savings size by 2021 – the sweet-spot ideal for the stock position. Of these eight, five are part of the Bay of Bengal group (India, Bangladesh, Vietnam, Indonesia and Nepal). Other Bay of Bengal markets like Thailand, Myanmar and Sri Lanka also lie in the periphery with high expected savings rates and high economic growth.

Stock apart, even flow is critical

Despite all the discussions about the savings stock, the current flow cannot be ignored as a measure of purchasing power of the people. How does one look at varied incomes across occupations and profiles? A worker in the technology sector may have seen better income growth in recent years than a worker in an industrial plant. Similarly, a graduate with an Ivy-League university degree may have seen better growth than a high-school pass-out. Hence for ease of comparison across countries as a whole, the average per capita income is taken as the measure of the flow of income growth each year. This has its obvious limitations, but it provides a quick comparison on a cross-country and cross-occupation basis.

As per the IMF'S WEO data of PPP GDP, a better comparison for purchasing power between countries, the expected per capita income growth till 2021 is taken as the proxy for the flow income. The CAGR growth rate of per capita till 2021 is 8% for the Bay of Bengal group (8% for BIMSTEC alone as well). This is the maximum from amongst the groups under study. This is followed by 7.5% for BRICS (although BRICS ex China ranks much lower with only a 5% CAGR). SAARC, NEXT 11, CIVETS and MINT follow with East Africa and Pacific Alliance close behind. The remaining groups like East Europe, GCC and CIS lag at around 4% CAGR. The median CAGR across all these regions is 5%. The Bay of Bengal group leads the pack by far.

Moreover, the range of the per capita income within the members is less in the case of the Bay of Bengal than it is in the ASEAN. This means that a similar basket of products can find takers across most of the member countries since they all have a similar profile, and hence aspiration. Conversely, a group like ASEAN where the per capita of Singapore or Malaysia is vastly different from Laos, Myanmar, Vietnam or Cambodia. That means vastly different aspirations (and products to meet those aspirations). This can also impact the grouping's market-size opportunity for a specific business.

Most importantly, the growth trajectories in the individual Bay of Bengal markets from now till 2021 share a high degree of synchronisation and linearity amongst themselves. This has been discussed in the earlier chapter on Asset Class. Essentially, this means that most of the markets are expected to grow on a similar track, and there are no major outliers. In comparison, the BRICS has severe outliers because South Africa, Russia and Brazil's growth trend has diverged from that of China and India. This is a critical reason to look at the Bay of Bengal markets as a group.

But has the per capita income in the Bay of Bengal group reached a meaningful size? According to the average per capita income data in the IMF's WEO, the Bay of Bengal group today is roughly where the BRICS was a decade ago, i.e. approximately US$2000 in Bay of Bengal (and BIMSTEC alone) in 2016 vs. US$ 2000 in BRICS in 2006, as per the IMF's WEO data on per capita. This was when a plethora of BRICS dedicated funds entered the investment industry, as they thought this level of average income adequate to drive the demand for businesses. Moreover, this number is double of what BRICS was back in 2001, i.e. US$1000, when the term BRIC was first coined by Goldman Sachs. It is also worth noting that the last decade has seen a divergence between BRICS and BRICS ex China groups, since China has become disproportionately wealthier than the rest.

Back in 2001, the per capita of the BRICS had grown at a decadal CAGR of 9% from 1991 to 2001, although this dipped to a 6% CAGR for the last five-years from 1996 to 2001. In comparison, the Bay of Bengal group's per capita has grown at a CAGR of 7% since the last decade from 2006, and the momentum has been maintained at a 6.5% CAGR even for the last five-years from 2011 to 2016. This holds true even for the BIMSTEC group alone. The estimate till 2021 for this group is 8%, higher than any of the others under study. In comparison, the growth estimate for the BRICS back in 2001 for the next year itself, i.e. 2002, was a mere 4%.

As economies mature and personal surplus expands, discretionary spending typically comprises a larger share, both in business production and in people's consumption basket. If the level of per capita income indicates a threshold level for increasing the discretionary spending, then this Bay of Bengal group is ideally poised to take off just like the BRICS was then. Are these per capita comparisons between the BRICS of a decade ago to the Bay of Bengal of today valid to demonstrate a threshold level of income acceptable for a group? May be or maybe not, since the nature of the growth and inflation levels has changed.

But looking at this group now on a standalone basis, then all countries making up the Bay of Bengal group have seen, and are expected to see, healthy growth, coupled with a reasonable homogeneity in their per capita levels. That makes the near-term future of this group optimistic.

Stock and flow apart, even distribution is critical

The quest for purchasing power does not end with stock and flow alone, the spread of that money also matters? So does income concentration expand the market opportunity? This is best explained by the market size vs. market share debate. Businesses have always had to choose between market share and market size. Which battle has to be fought depends on how much of the potential consumer base it has tapped, how big is the addressable consumer base and how many players are competing. Based on this, it has to choose whether it should target the market size or market share. Specific sectors in the same country can show varying pictures. This book is looking at developing countries, most of whom are typically under-penetrated in several business sectors. For instance, their penetration of cars, housing, appliances and other products is still low, relative to their consumer base. So from the perspective of an overall country, it may be prudent to first focus on the market size. So how many people in these countries have an adequate level of income that can help the business' penetration further in that market? The level of income distribution can give a clue. If income is spread across more hands, it offers a wider opportunity for product penetration; and so businesses should focus on the market size. If income is spread across fewer hands, it offers limited opportunity for product penetration across a wider customer base; and so businesses should focus on grabbing market share of those few customers from the competitors. Yes, the actual income would matter for individual products; but the idea here is to look at the overall picture as a whole.

The under-penetrated sectors of these countries form the major rationale for businesses to look at these markets. Pushing these sectors will generate growth, employment and income in the coming years. Hence, the talk of the spread of income and the opportunity to drive market size – often a more profitable opportunity for businesses than the cut-throat pricing that accompanies market share battles. In such markets where the penetration of many products is still very low, it may be better if more people have a share of the income in that country, so that the potential consumer base of that product is wider. However, if only a few people in that country have a share of the income in that country, then the potential consumer base is restricted to only those people, and the resultant battle for businesses will be to grab market share of those few consumers.

The World Bank's Gini coefficient data shows a country's income concentration. A lower coefficient indicates that the income of the country is spread across more people. A higher coefficient number indicates that the wealth of the country is concentrated in the hands of only a few people. Countries like Brazil and South Africa, part of the BRICS group, have very high coefficient numbers near 60, as per the latest data available on World Bank's Gini coefficient. This indicates the money in these countries is held in few hands. This high concentration restricts the potential size of the consumer base for many products. The majority poor cannot demand many products, while the few rich will only demand certain affluent products. Those products will fight to grab market share from amongst those few rich individuals. Even countries like Chile, Nigeria, Kenya, Colombia, Peru, Mexico, Saudi Arabia, Singapore, Peru, Qatar, Malaysia, Turkey, China and the Philippines have a relatively high level of income concentration, with their Gini coefficient figures hovering in the 40–50 range. Countries like Thailand, Indonesia, Russia, Bhutan, Myanmar, Sri Lanka, Cambodia, Vietnam, India, Nepal, Taiwan, Ethiopia, Poland, Bangladesh, South Korea, Romania and Pakistan all have a relatively lower level of income concentration, with their Gini coefficient figures hovering in the 30–40 range. This indicates that the wealth in these countries is spread across more hands. All nine markets of the Bay of Bengal group fall in this category. This expands the potential consumer base for many products that are starting to see penetration in those markets.

Back in 2001, the BRICS countries like Brazil and South Africa had high Gini coefficient figures; indicating income inequality has remained chronic in these countries. South Africa and Brazil were at an extreme with numbers over 60 – a very high coefficient indeed. Since then, programmes like Bolsa Brazil and government transfers helped reduce income inequality in Brazil to some extent, but it still remains on the higher side. With income inequality so high in these countries, many businesses would struggle to widen their market size and would end up in market share battles, which can often be detrimental for corporate profitability due to price-wars.

For the groups collectively, the average for the Pacific Alliance (simple average of the individual countries' figures) was the highest at 48, followed by BRICS ex China, BRICS, GCC, MINT, Africa (Big Economies), CIVETS and ASEAN with average scores above 40. They are followed by NEXT 11, MENA, BIMSTEC, Bay of Bengal, SAARC and the East Europe groups, with average scores between 30 and 40. Not only is the Bay of Bengal group on the lower-end on the income concentration scale, it is also far below the average of the MSCI EM Index group. In short, the income is spread across a wider base of people in this group, which augurs well for the market size opportunity of many products. Widening the market size can offer a large opportunity for many products in these markets in the coming years. A simple-average methodology may not take into account the exact weightage of the countries within the group, since their size varies. Nevertheless, it is only used for indicative purpose. In the groups with a higher average coefficient, grabbing the market share of the few rich from incumbent competitors forms the bulk of the opportunity for many products.

A look at the wealth concentration amongst countries can give further insights on the distribution of the overall wealth, rather than just income. However, that is not included here since exact country-wise data for all the countries in this sample-set is not publicly available. Nevertheless, that can be an interesting addition in this context.

Of course, every country will also have disparities within its provinces when it comes to income and affluence. Malaysia makes an interesting case in terms of the economic disparity between Peninsula Malaysia and the Borneo island in eastern Malaysia. On a trip to Kota Kinabalu, the capital of Sabah, one of the two provinces in the Malaysian portion of Borneo island, it was surprising to see a passport-control immigration line at the airport for even the domestic flights from Peninsula Malaysia. Official reasons may be what they are; but my inkling while travelling around the city was that limiting labour migration was probably one of the reasons. Unlike Peninsula Malaysian cities where work opportunities are relatively in good supply, there were gaps here. The province itself is not as affluent as Peninsula Malaysia, based on the observations of the cleanliness of the roads, relatively less crowd thronging its city-centre malls, aimless youth in market-areas or ladies soliciting in the garb of massage parlours. Malaysia's Department of Statistics data shows that the unemployment rate of Sabah was 5.4% vs. 3.4% for Malaysia as a whole, a 60% difference. Sabah's unemployment rate was the highest amongst all the Malaysian provinces, barring the small island of the Labuan federal region. With fewer jobs and less income, Sabah's differences with Peninsula Malaysia were stark. So for a country which already has a high level of income concentration, the relative disparity of affluence amongst its prosperous and poorer regions would be an additional factor dictating which opportunity works better – market size or market share.

In conclusion, this chapter has looked at some of the critical components of a country's purchasing power, i.e. the stock of savings, the flow of income, the size of per capita and the distribution of money amongst the population. The findings give some evidence to say that this group is snugly placed on all three fronts. There are challenges, especially to India's savings growth. On the whole, the estimates augur well for the long term market opportunity for businesses looking at the Bay of Bengal group; and for the investors invested in those businesses, ultimately feeding the group's rationale to be a regional asset class in itself.

Building for Tomorrow
The Investment Story

Based on my travels in all the regional countries, it may be safe to say that Sri Lanka is an exception in the South Asian region. This is in context of the quality of urban infrastructure and civic amenities. The state of the roads tells a lot about the efficiency of a country, as do serpentine lines in the airports and railway stations. After all, these are the first things any visitor sees, and it creates their first and last impression (literally and metaphorically). The roads in Colombo, the capital city of Sri Lanka, are a treat to eyes otherwise made sore travelling throughout South Asia, where pothole-ridden roads, broken sidewalks and long unlit stretches in most metro cities abound. In Colombo, all traffic lights work; and more importantly, they are followed by the drivers instead of being relegated to being mere ornaments. Footpaths are built conveniently to walk even in the narrowest of streets, and pedestrians do not have to step onto the actual road like they inevitably have to do in certain stretches in Indian cities like Mumbai, Delhi, etc., thus endangering themselves in the direct line of the traffic. Moreover, this entire urban landscape in Colombo is without any major flyovers, negating the excuse of many cities that the absence of flyovers limits their ability to solve traffic woes. Not just in downtown Colombo, this quality of urban infrastructure is visible even in its suburbs as well as in other towns like Kandy and Galle.

Yes, maintenance of roads and traffic also requires the citizens' attitude to follow those rules, something lacking amongst many people in the South Asian countries. Whilst on a visit to the British town of York few years ago, it was surprising to see cars stop at the traffic lights even at 3 a.m. in the morning when the roads were empty. It is tough to see this level of adherence to traffic rules in most South Asian countries at 3 p.m. in the afternoon, let alone at 3 a.m. in the morning. However, I saw this occur in Colombo while on my way to the Fort station at 5 a.m. Also, with good quality urban infrastructure bringing in its own semblance of safety, it is no wonder that one can see Sri Lankan women of all ages comfortably walking along the streets even at late-hours in the night, something their counterparts in most South Asian cities may not be so comfortable doing.

Critics of this observation can argue that the small population and size of Colombo (and even of Sri Lanka) relative to the other South Asian countries allows it to invest better into the quality of urban infrastructure. That argument has its merits; but then Sri Lanka is also a much smaller economy than its regional peers and hence has far less resources to invest in its public services. So on a proportionate basis, it may yet be an apple to apple comparison. This also highlights that Sri Lanka invested those scanty resources more appropriately than the other regional countries, since the difference in the results is stark and visible.

The ideal investment rate

The IMF's WEO data of the share of investments to GDP of more than two-dozen countries comprising key emerging markets and regional neighbours may offer some analogy to the current state of Sri Lankan infrastructure. Back in the 1990s when the Southeast and East Asian economies like South Korea, Malaysia, Thailand and Indonesia had jumped on the investment bandwagon, their average investment to GDP rates from 1993 to 1997 was close to 35–40%, even crossing 40% in some cases like Malaysia and Thailand. This was the time when these Asian markets had gone on an investment spree to fuel their export-oriented industries. Incidentally much of these investments were not adequately backed by domestic savings, forcing them to take external borrowings. The pressure of falling exports on the back of a rise in Thailand's then pegged-currency, excessive investment and the repayment of borrowings and imports all combined to trigger the 1997 Asian currency crisis. The situation is very different now, but the scale of investment that took place in those early years is partly a reason why the quality of urban infrastructure, roads and highways across Southeast Asia is of a far superior quality than most South Asian countries. Forget their main cities, my travels in the interiors of countries like Thailand, Malaysia, Indonesia and even

Cambodia, showed that the quality of their highways and suburban-roads is as good as their main city-roads. Such quality can be seen only in certain stretches of India, even today.

Even the BRICS ex China group countries are a contrast to Southeast Asia. The average investment rate in the BRICS ex China & India group collectively was only 20% in 2016, although this was higher at 25% for the BRICS ex China grouping and a high of 38% for the BRICS as a whole. So any traction in the BRICS has been led largely by China, which maintained a 40% plus investment rate for most of the 1990s and 2000s. The stark difference between Chinese infrastructure with those in India or Brazil is there for all to see. As many as seven of the ten largest container ports in the world by goods traffic are in China (Ningbo, Shenzhen, Tianjin, Qingdao, Guangzhou, Hong Kong and Shanghai), and each of them manages traffic which is about 3–10x higher than the largest ports of India and Brazil (Mumbai and Santos respectively). That is what investment can create! Incidentally, the port in Sri Lanka's Colombo handled more container traffic than India's Mumbai in 2016.

Given these experiences in Southeast Asia and China, it may seem that maintaining an investment rate in the range of 35–40% in the initial years of a country's development journey may be deemed ideal. This may indicate the extent by which any country or region should seek to raise their investment rate if they want to pass through a similar evolution. Once the country progresses along that journey, it may taper this to below 35–40% or maybe further towards 30% to avoid unproductive excesses.

Are countries investing more or less

In Sri Lanka, the average investment rate increased by as much as 300 base points between the successive five-year periods of 2011 to 2016 and 2006 to 2011, as per the IMF'S WEO data. This is one of the highest increases amongst the larger economies of the Bay of Bengal group, along with Indonesia, Myanmar, Bhutan and Nepal, apart from Malaysia, China and the Philippines. On the other hand, group countries like India and Vietnam have seen this metric dip. Not only these two, but many large emerging markets have curtailed their investments, including Nigeria, Mexico, Poland, Romania, South Africa, Brazil and Pakistan – despite many continuing to suffer from a chronic shortage of infrastructure. This is probably one of the reasons why the transformation in Sri Lanka's infrastructure quality is so discernible now.

From the late 1980s to the mid-1990s, most Southeast Asian countries also demonstrated this trend between their average investments rates, to the extent that Malaysia has seen an uptick of as high as a 1000 base points. Even China experienced this. The traction in Sri Lanka perhaps highlights its government's commitment to improve its infrastructure. Amongst the others, Nepal might be deemed an exception, as much of its investments have gone to rebuild its existing infrastructure after earthquakes. Bhutan and Myanmar are still in a very early-stage of their development, hence will see the initial ramp up in energy and infrastructure. There is also reason to debate whether China and Malaysia are over-doing their investments just to hit a threshold growth each year, as they have reached a certain level of development. Bangladesh, Indonesia and the Philippines perhaps make better comparisons to Sri Lanka.

Apart from the increase in investment rate, Sri Lanka's investment as a proportion to GDP has been above 30% in five out of the six years from 2011 and 2016. Excluding Sri Lanka, only China, India, Indonesia, Bhutan and Nepal from the two-dozen markets under study clocked an investment rate of 30% plus in these six years. Apart from these, the average rate in Bangladesh, Vietnam, South Korea, Romania, Saudi Arabia and Turkey hovered in the late-20s for this period. This was even lower in other markets (some being notable emerging markets) like Poland, Mexico, Brazil, Russia, South Africa, Pakistan, Nigeria, Colombia, Thailand, Malaysia, Kenya, the UAE and the Philippines. So while Sri Lanka's 30% plus investment rate was not close to the near-40% seen in Southeast Asia or China, it is still amongst the higher ones in the sample. Hence, it fared better in comparison to the other larger South Asian economies like India, Bangladesh and Pakistan.

Apart from intent, even usage is important. Intent defines the plan while usage defines the execution. Plan and execution have to go together for the investment to succeed. So did the investment go into infrastructure like building assets, or did it go into comparatively unproductive avenues? As per a Sri Lankan central bank report on 'Economic and Social Infrastructure', its government's investments in infrastructure in the economic services segment grew at a staggering 24% CAGR during the five-years from 2006 to 2011, which coincides with the 500 base points uptick seen in its average investment rate between the successive five-year periods of 2006 to 2011 and 2001 to 2006. That trend should ideally have continued in the current decade as well.

On the other hand, investment to GDP in Bangladesh is lower than most South Asian neighbours (with the exception of Pakistan which has a sub-20% rate); and most investments have probably gone into its garment exports apparatus. While this situation is still a productive investment since garments make up over three-fourths of its exports, it possibly meant less inflow into urban infrastructure development in its cities. Only recently has this issue come under intense focus in Dhaka, and some new flyovers have come up in Dhaka's northern suburbs. But do these differences in usage help explain the state of Colombo's roads relative to the region?

So how are the markets of the Bay of Bengal group faring on investments? Are they building enough capacity for tomorrow? Deficient infrastructure implies that supply ultimately may not be able to cope with an increase in demand, which will only add supply-side pressures to inflation; something not even monetary policy can adequately address. India's experience with inflation during 2012–2014 is an example. It will push up the final cost of the product, while creating fewer jobs than what large population countries desperately need.

As per the IMF's WEO data projections, the Bay of Bengal group collectively had an average investment rate of 35% back in 2011, which dipped to 30% in 2016. It is expected to increase only marginally to 31% by 2021. BIMSTEC's would be 30%. Even then, it is far below what should be the ideal number, if one goes by the ideal 35–40% seen in Southeast Asia and China during their initial stages of development. The main culprit is India.

Along with China, Brazil and Nigeria, India's average investment rate for the five years till 2021 is expected to slip as compared to the preceding five years. The drop is estimated to be as high as 500 base points in India's case, one of the steepest. This is a critical challenge in a country that is trying to push up domestic manufacturing. No other country in this group is on such a sticky wicket. Bangladesh, Indonesia and Sri Lanka are expected to maintain a 30% plus investment rate through the next five years. So even while Bangladesh had an investment rate only in the late-20s, it is expected to go up by 200 base points over the five years till 2021, as compared to its preceding five-year average. This will place its average investment rate in 2021 only behind China, Indonesia, Sri Lanka, Bhutan and Nepal, from the countries under study. India's investment rate is less than the threshold for countries in early stages of development. Its government is now making the right noises to scale this up with a new infrastructure fund. That is a positive. Southeast Asian countries like Thailand, Indonesia, Vietnam and Myanmar, part of the Bay of Bengal group, are better placed. The expectation is that their average investment rates will be largely maintained till 2021. Indonesia is seeing an investment rate close to 35%, while Vietnam's is close to 30%.

Amongst the other groups, BRICS leads the pack with an expected investment rate of 36% in 2021, down from 38% in 2016. MENA would be at 30%, ASEAN, CIVETS and SAARC at 29% each, NEXT 11 and MINT at 28% each, East Africa at 27%, Pacific Alliance at 24%, East Europe at 23% and BRICS ex China & India at 20%. The MSCI EM Index as a whole is expected to reach a level of 25%. The maximum appreciation between 2016 and 2021 would be seen in MENA, BIMSTEC ex India and NEXT 11.

Investing in manufacturing, not just infrastructure

In this narrative, the focus so far has been on infrastructure as the outcome of investment. Manufacturing is another outcome of investments. Manufacturing needs investments in plants and machineries, in roads to reach to those plants, in ports to take that produce to the wider market, and a whole virtuous cycle of incomes and jobs and services sector like transport, housing, retail trade and finance follows. This push towards manufacturing was a key factor that enabled the success stories of development to emerge – from the USA, Europe and Japan during the industrial revolution; to South Korea, Malaysia, Taiwan and Singapore in the 20th century's export-oriented growth; till China in the 21st century's manufacturing super-power.

So does a high rate of investment in a country coincide with a higher share of industry in the economy, relative to the share of services and agriculture? CIA World Factbook and the IMF's WEO data shows that the gap between the share of industry within the economy in 2016 and the average investment rate over the last decade (assuming it takes at least 10 years of investment to construct a reasonable scale of facilities) were largely similar in the case of Sri Lanka. It was similar even in the case of Vietnam. This gap has been a high-negative in India as well as Kenya and Nepal, perhaps demonstrating to some extent the misplaced usage of the investments in those countries. On the other hand, this gap is a high-positive in South Korea, Indonesia, Thailand, Malaysia, Romania and Poland, perhaps demonstrating the improvement that occurs in the productivity of investments over time, considering these countries have been investing for a substantial period since the 1990s. South Asian countries like India, Nepal and Bhutan have some catching-up to do in terms of the contribution of industry to their economies.

So India is a laggard here as well; and this is a major challenge for this Bay of Bengal group since the absolute investments of India make up half of that of the group's. The share of industry to its output is lagging relative to the other markets under study, and it is ahead only of Pakistan, Kenya, Brazil, Nepal and Nigeria. The good news is that some of its infrastructure projects like national highway network are progressing at a good pace; and even the construction of modern ports has come under intense focus.

To what extent can investments boost economic output

This is an important question for those in India who feel domestic consumption is an adequate driver of economic growth, since India has relied on consumption excessively in recent years. What is the multiplier-effect of investments to output? To get some idea of what this multiplier-effect can potentially be, let us take the Southeast Asian economies in the 1990s. The combined national output of South Korea, Malaysia, Indonesia and Thailand grew at a 13% CAGR for the decade from the late-1980s till 1997. During this period, their combined investments in absolute amount grew at a 10% CAGR, with bulk of the addition naturally coming in the initial years of the decade for it to turn productive. This simple extrapolation indicates a potential 1.3x impact. Looking at China's case, extrapolating the data of the preceding decade till the 2008 crisis saw a 1x relationship between growth in investment and output. In short, the potential multiplier impact seems to be in the range of 1–1.3x.

How do the two-dozen countries under study, especially the Bay of Bengal nations, perform on this front? The CAGR in GDP over the last five years vs. the CAGR in investments shows that amongst the countries which saw a positive GDP growth, only Vietnam, Sri Lanka, China and Kenya ranked within the 1–1.3x multiplier impact bracket, indicating productive usage of investments. Two of these are part of the Bay of Bengal group, including Sri Lanka – the country which is an exception in South Asia when it comes to investment.

This multiplier is slightly less in Pakistan, Indonesia, Myanmar, Nigeria, Bhutan, Bangladesh and the Philippines, indicating their investment needs to be used more productively. Some of these are part of the Bay of Bengal group. Conversely, this multiplier is negative in India, Malaysia, Romania, Turkey, Thailand and the UAE, indicating their investments have been used largely counter-productively in this period. Of course, the GDP of a country is impacted by a myriad other factors apart from investments, so this cannot be an exact comparison. Nonetheless, it does offer fodder for relative comparison and discussion.

The Bay of Bengal group remains a mixed bag – some countries have to invest more while others have to improve the productivity of their investments. For the group as a whole, the expected GDP growth collectively till 2021 is 9%. The expected growth in the Bay of Bengal group's investments till 2021 is also 9%, which gives an investment to GDP multiplier of 1x (same for BIMSTEC alone). This is on the lower end of the 1–1.3x scale seen from the Southeast Asian and Chinese experiences. This reaffirms that improving the productivity and quantum of the investments is a challenge in this group.

Incremental growth is an incentive to ramp up investment

But despite the funding challenges, there exists a big incentive to ramp up investment further over the coming years. Global growth is getting redistributed incrementally, and this is an incentive for countries that invested inadequately to invest further and capture this opportunity. Growth alone does not matter, size also counts. Size matters since it indicates the appetite that the opportunity can absorb. A market like East Africa may be fast growing, but its relatively small size restricts the absolute amount of opportunities (and hence, investments) it can absorb. That will limit investor interest beyond a point. A market like the Bay of Bengal group, which is growing at a high rate and also expected to add a size as big as BRICS ex China, would have a larger appetite for investments, since it has to fuel more growth in absolute terms.

To talk about the BRICS, its contribution to the incremental global output for the five-years from 2002 to 2007 was about US$5 billion. It made up 21% of the incremental pie, which was double its contribution from 1996 to 2001. During this period, the contribution of the G-7 nations to the incremental global output had been 40%, exactly half from what it was from 1996 to 2001. That shows the distribution of incremental economic output between the 1990s and 2000s. However, the last five-years from 2011 to 2016 saw global economic growth taper off to a CAGR of only 0.6%. Within this 0.6% CAGR, the G-7 countries grew at a 0.3% CAGR, the MSCI EM Index countries grew at a 2% CAGR, the Bay of Bengal group at a 4% CAGR and BRICS at a 3% CAGR while BRICS ex China faltered with a negative 4% CAGR. This meant that the Bay of Bengal group saw its contribution to incremental global output cross 30% (27% for BIMSTEC alone), up from the 5% a decade earlier from 2002 to 2007. This indicates some distribution of incremental economic output towards this group.

The incremental size added by the BRICS ex China is expected to be US$2.5 billion from 2016 to 2021, and the Bay of Bengal group is also expected to add a similar incremental size of US$2.2 billion. In short, both groups are expected to add the same size incrementally till 2021 as growth gets further distributed. BIMSTEC alone is expected to add $1.6 billion incrementally by 2021, NEXT 11 will add $2.4 billion, MINT $1.3 billion, SAARC $1.6 billion, East Europe and CIVETS $1.1 billion each, MENA and ASEAN $1.2 billion each and Pacific Alliance and Africa (Big Economies) will add $0.6 billion each. The MSCI EM Index grouping as a whole is expected to add $5.7 billion incrementally by 2021.

If one looks at overall economic size instead of the incremental pieces, the Bay of Bengal group was larger in size in 2016 than what the BRICS was back in 2001 – US$4 billion vs. US$2.8 billion. The overall size of US$6 billion expected of the Bay of Bengal group by 2021 is equivalent to where the BRICS had reached by 2006, i.e. five years after the term BRIC was coined. Moreover, the growth rates now are not as high as they were in the 2000s. So is the Bay of Bengal group large enough to be an incentive to boost the investment rate?

But the competition has also gone up at the same time – another reason for ramping up investments. Regions that were smaller back in the 2000s as far as their contribution to the incremental pie was concerned are also growing. Incremental growth is migrating to those places too, and the incremental investor interest may follow suit. For instance, the ASEAN is expected to contribute over 5% of the incremental global output between 2016 and 2021, up from 3% a decade ago. Similarly, the Next-11 will contribute 11%, up from 9% and the Pacific Alliance group will add 3%, up from 2%. The East Africa region (including Ethiopia) may be expected to comprise only 0.5% of the incremental pie, but this is more than double of its 0.2% share a decade ago.

But will all these incremental investments create over-capacity eventually, especially if global growth remains muted? Can pushing the investment rate too far end up creating a bubble in the 2020s, the source of the next big crisis? The chance of this occurring in the Bay of Bengal group is less as of now, since the absolute stock of infrastructure and plants still remains far from the basic desired levels. There are still a lot of roads and bridges to be built. That journey augurs well from the perspective of avoiding an imminent situation of over-capacity due to excess investment, at least on the infrastructure side if not on the manufacturing side. This issue would rather worry those countries that continue to maintain excessively high rates of investments despite reaching a certain level of industrialisation, like Malaysia or China. The bigger threat of capacity in the Bay of Bengal markets will be from the perspective of their inability to compete with cheaper imports from such over-capacitated countries, which will be desperate to find new markets to maintain their growth. Some of this is already happening now and is a pressing threat, since it reduces the imminent urgency to invest into local infrastructure and manufacturing capabilities.

Funding the investments

But expectations of investment growth raise another question – where are these investments going to be funded from? Excessive external borrowings taken up to fund investments were partly to blame for the 1997 Asian currency crisis. This situation is different now, as the gap between the investment and the saving rates has been closed, so that the pressure to resort to external borrowings is minimal. Most of the Bay of Bengal group countries excel on this front. A positive differential between the average savings rate and the average investment rate till 2021 is expected in Thailand, Vietnam, South Korea, Russia and the UAE, from amongst the countries under study. It is marginally positive for Nepal, Saudi Arabia, Malaysia and China.

In all, three of these countries are part of the Bay of Bengal group. A very high positive differential is also undesirable, since it indicates savings are not being used productively. So it probably raises a new worry of excess savings. That bridge can be crossed once reached! Returning to the worry of less-than adequate savings to fund the required level of investment, this differential is marginally negative in India, Bangladesh, Brazil, Indonesia, Sri Lanka, Poland and the Philippines. Four are part of the Bay of Bengal group. A negative gap between expected domestic saving and investment means they have to resort to external borrowings; but since the gap is only marginal, it means the extent of external borrowings should be limited. Ergo, the pressure on deficits should be limited. On the other hand, this gap is wider for Pakistan, Turkey, Romania, Kenya, Bhutan, Myanmar, Colombia, South Africa and Mexico. Two are part of the Bay of Bengal group, and this is worrying. The only solace is that they are smaller-sized economies; hence the deficit pressure on the overall group is limited.

Typically, developing nations will also see a spike in imports coinciding with a spike in investments in their early stages. In Sri Lanka, import comprised ~30% of its GDP, which is similar to its share of investment. The experience of recent industrializing nations shows that the share of imports is typically about ~50–60% of their share of investment. This means part of Sri Lanka's imports may have been for non-productive purposes. On the other hand, imports comprised ~20% of Bangladesh's GDP, another Bay of Bengal group country. This is ~60% of its share of gross investment, which is same as that seen in recent industrializing nations. So Sri Lanka has to reduce its share of unproductive imports, while Bangladesh has to continue this trend. The smaller South Asian nations like Nepal and Bhutan also fall in the same league as Sri Lanka, as their share of imports to GDP is equal to their share of investments. Looking at the Southeast Asian example of Indonesia, its import comprised ~18% of its GDP, which is roughly half of its share of investment. Hence, Indonesia's case is in line with that seen in recent industrializing nations, just like Bangladesh.

So apart from the external borrowing, even the pressure of import cost is a cost of investment since one also has to fund the machineries and capital goods imported to build those infrastructure and plants. Most developing countries do not have domestic expertise to produce these machineries locally, hence some imports are inevitable. If exports are high, it helps net off the demand for foreign exchange for imports to some extent. Large importers in the Bay of Bengal group like Bangladesh and Vietnam were able to net off their import cost with robust export growth in the last five years till 2016, which helped them maintain a positive current account surplus, a surprise amongst developing countries.

This gap in net exports was moderately worrisome for India, Thailand and Indonesia, while it was far more worrisome for Pakistan, Sri Lanka, Myanmar, Bhutan and the Philippines, where exports fell severely short of imports. Three of these countries are part of the Bay of Bengal group. An equal challenge to ramp up investments will be to contain current deficits, especially in countries seeing a high growth in imports to fund investments.

On India specifically, the main laggard in the group, it has put in place some initiatives to mobilize funding to meet the cost of investments without resorting to high-cost loans from other countries. It has started its new infrastructure fund, NIIF, to mobilize monies from institutional investors like pension funds and sovereign wealth funds to meet its infrastructure cost. This fund is evincing initial interest.

The government also implemented innovative fund-raising methods like the exchange traded fund (ETF) for public sector enterprises (PSE) disinvestment, and this is showing positive contribution. It has launched two ETF products to divest part of the government's stake in certain public sector enterprises, and thus help raise fiscal revenues. These two ETFs are the C-PSE ETF and the Bharat 22 ETF. ETF are just like any fund, which raises monies from the retail public and institutions and invests it in securities for investment gains. In this case, the shares it buys in the offer are those hitherto held with the government. Being an ETF, it is listed on the exchanges unlike an open-ended mutual fund. That enables further trading by investors and viewing of daily pricing. Bharat 22, the latest PSE ETF fund launched at end-2016, invests in the stocks of 22 PSEs across six sectors - finance, energy, industrials, materials, FMCG, and utilities. A sector cap of 20% and a stock cap of 15% help manage the exposure risk. The stocks are selected based on their underlying fundamental performance and their potential to gain from sector-based reforms. The first PSE ETF invested in the stocks of ten PSEs. As per India's Department of Investment and Public Asset Management, Bharat 22 ETF raised Rs. 145 billion in its initial offer, making up almost one-third of the actual disinvestment achieved till-date in the year. This indicates the level of investor interest in the product. As of January 2018, the Rs. 145 billion Bharat 22 ETF had been the single-largest source of disinvestment so far for the fiscal year 2017–18; and it has a significant lead over the next largest sources, i.e. the NTPC and GIC issuances of Rs. 90 billion each. Is this route workable only for PSEs with better-performing fundamentals? Possibly, as investing presupposes that better performers will be in the radar, but this is an incomplete view. India's government-owned banks were amongst the worst performers owing to asset quality concerns. However, the Bharat 22 ETF does hold stakes in government-owned banks. At the same time, the opportunity cost also has to be considered. One motive of raising lump sum revenues is to utilize it for large-scale asset creation which would yield value in the long term. This type of lump sum revenues is not possible from the dividends the government earns each year from them. Moreover, direct divestment through a strategic sale has not always shown results. However, this ETF product now offers a solution by divesting smaller stakes across multiple investors, and contributing to fiscal revenue which can be used to fund further investment.

In conclusion, this chapter has looked at how various regions compare in terms of ramping up their investment levels over the last decade and the extent to which it can impact economic output. It compares if investment has gone more into investment or manufacturing, and why there is an incentive for the Bay of Bengal group countries to ramp up investments now.

The Mix and the Journey
The Sector Story

During a trip to Chennai in 2017 to give some guest-lectures, my car passed several glass and grey-tiled buildings while travelling from the airport to a university in the city's southern suburbs. It was the typical façade of modern Corporate India buildings as seen in many of its cities, which are often the delivery-centres of technology or offshoring companies. It was a working-day at about 9 a.m. in the morning at that time, yet the crowd of employees and vehicles entering those buildings seemed far less as compared to the size of the buildings. Granted that many technology and offshoring companies operate night or late-shifts which would reduce the morning-shift crowd or perhaps the building was running huge vacancy rates, nevertheless the crowd entering those buildings seemed too small even then. Spending most of my corporate career in similar office buildings in Gurgaon and Mumbai had helped build a fair estimate of how populous the office-crowd should be to the scale of the building. Later that day, while passing similar glass grey-tiled buildings while travelling to another university in the city-centre, the crowd of employees and vehicles entering those building at that time, presumably the afternoon-shift employees, still seemed far less than what it should be.

Towards evening, while passing the city's commercial hubs of Anna Salai and T Nagar, the office-crowd in those areas seemed as populous as they have always been. The evening rush hour of office-goers had just started; hence it was easy to see the stream of employees leaving the various office buildings there. These areas housed a more traditional mix of businesses, like banks and offices of industrial groups, unlike the technology centric companies that housed most of the glass and grey-tiled buildings in the suburbs. So why was it that the glass grey-tiled office complexes in the suburbs saw such sparse crowds, while commerce seemed to be flowing as vibrantly as ever in the traditional office areas?

While chatting in those universities about my observation, it seemed that most of the companies that had come there for job placements in recent years to pick up graduating students were from the financial and retail companies, unlike the technology companies who used to pick up the maximum number of students earlier. After returning to Mumbai, the research analysts to whom the question was asked about which sectors were doing well or weren't, said that technology, India's bellwether sector, was struggling. This sector had earned it global laurels and shareholder dividends since the last couple of decades, but was now undergoing headwinds. Changes in new technologies globally and the resultant shifts in client needs had posed fresh challenges to Indian software companies, many of whom were still struggling to migrate their service offerings to the newer, complex technologies. They had thrived so far on their vanilla software outsourcing, but times were changing. The ones unable to adapt quickly were facing cost pressures, resulting in downsizing and fewer hires. That partly explained the lesser crowds seen entering those glass and grey-tiled buildings at office hour.

Eyewitness accounts and analyst views can be one-off at times; hence data offers further observation. Bloomberg data of absolute profits earned by the largest 200 listed companies by sectors from 2012 to 2016 showed that while the larger technology sector companies in India had collectively grown their average profit per company over those last five years, the traction was largely due to two giants only (TCS and HCL). If the numbers of those two giants were removed, the rest were in troubled waters in terms of their average profit per company. If economic stories are ephemeral, then sector stories are even more so. Technology had comprised 16% of the total profit pool of the largest 200 listed Indian companies by 2016 market cap, up from 8% five years ago. However, it seemed the current financial year might see a hit. Finance and energy had been the two largest sectors in India's profit pool, followed by technology. Technology had displaced the materials sector in 2013 to take the third spot since then. However, its position now faces a threat. This comparison looks at profits because that is one of the main items an investor looks at. Profitability has become a more stringent yardstick for evaluating corporate and market performance in the post-2008 world.

But other countries are picking up speed in these sectors. In Colombo's downtown Fort area, there is a twin-tower office complex called World Trade Centre. This complex houses, amongst others, offices of a few off-shoring companies. Some of these companies in Sri Lanka offer the same set of services that their counterparts in India did, and they now benefit from the increased migration of work from India because it is a more cost-effective alternative for those services. The north-eastern island of Penang in Malaysia is making its mark as a regional technology hub. Some years ago, Malaysia pushed its technology sector to Penang, in order to distribute the share of economic activities which were traditionally centred on the Selangor, Kuala Lumpur and Johor areas. Some locals even referred to Penang as the Silicon Valley of the East. In the southern fringes of Penang's capital Georgetown, a number of nouveau-design office buildings and accompanying apartment complexes can be seen, mostly housing its technology, electronics and offshoring offices. Some of these firms are working on new technologies, while some are working on traditional shared-services. Whichever the case, India faces growing competition already in both the traditional and new technology services space. The above narrative hints at gloom, but all is not doom for India. Yes, it is facing stress, but enterprising Indian tech-experts are working hard to make new break-throughs and offer a more relevant suite of services. That would make the players emerge as more relevant with more sustainable business models.

But this situation about India's technology sector raises three critical questions, which may be pertinent from the perspective of looking at the Bay of Bengal markets as an investible opportunity. Does a market's major sector change? Do specific sectors start contributing disproportionately to a market's profit pool as it matures? If so, could the journey towards further concentration in those new sectors be an investment opportunity? Lastly, is there a tipping-point beyond which these sectors may stop having a maximising impact on the overall economic growth?

Which sectors grow in prominence as a market matures

Bloomberg data of the sector-wise profits of the largest 200 listed companies by 2016 market capitalisation across major developing markets shows that certain sectors invariably grow in prominence as economies mature, and these sectors provide a rationale for investors. The data of the developed markets like the USA, UK, Japan, Canada and Germany is taken as a proxy for matured markets. After all, if something has not worked in the experience of the developed economies whose sector strengths should ideally have matured through their journey, then it probably would not work for developing economies either.

The profits of their largest 200 listed companies showed an uncanny tilt towards the consumer and industrial sectors, along with the financial sector. These three sectors comprised about three-fourths of Germany's 2016 profits. It was a similar number in Canada. In the UK, USA and Japan, this number was closer to 60%. The average for all the five together was nearer the two-thirds mark. Moreover, the proportions of these three top sectors have grown in all the five developed markets, between 2012 and 2016. This shows that concentration towards consumer and industrial sectors becomes inevitable beyond a point, as an economy matures. It hints that the trend is more structural than transitory.

But why would these few sectors emerge common across most of the matured markets? It cannot be a simple coincidence. This trend is possibly in line with the scaling up of discretionary consumer spending in countries as the disposable income of its people rises, along with scaling up and modernisation of their manufacturing sector to produce those consumer goods. These changes in the structure as an economy matures create the tendency for consumer driven businesses and the industrial infrastructure to flourish. Countries like Japan and Germany were strong exporters of industrial products, while the USA and UK were strong consumers.

Apart from identifying consumer, industrial and financial as the three sectors that rise in prominence in a market's profit pool as that economy matures, the other observation was the two-third mark – the typical threshold level its largest three sectors should ideally comprise.

Turning to the developing economies, every country has had their competitive advantage, which could be inherent or acquired. For instance, a nation like Qatar or Saudi Arabia had an inherent competitive advantage because they are located right on top of one of the world's largest known reserves of oil and gas. If geography ever offered pure luck, this is it. Nations in South Asia or East Asia, which did not have the luck of being located above major oil and gas reserves, had to work hard to build and acquire their areas of competitive advantage from scratch. Thus, the technology sector came up in India, textile in Bangladesh, cement in Pakistan and electronics manufacturing in the East Asian nations, etc. Malaysia is another example of an acquired competitive advantage, this time in the agro-sector. It is a global leader in palm oil production. Over the last century, the British colonizers of Malaysia saw the local climate was suited for palm growing. They imported cheap labour from India's Tamil-speaking regions, cleaned up vast swathes of land and created what would be Malaysia's key export for years to come. Even now, any plane landing at the Kuala Lumpur international airport in Selangor literally flies over hundreds of square kilometres of palm plantations for the last 15 minutes of the flight's descent. As such sectors of competitive advantage mature, the tendency of nations is to disproportionately invest more resources into those specific sectors, often ending up ignoring the others. These sectors keep on growing, thus making their share in the market more concentrated. This occurs till the sector reaches a tipping-point, when either the competitive advantage ends or a new change is needed in that competitive advantage.

China is the best example of a large developing country that has grown at a sustained rapid rate in recent decades. South Korea also grew at a sustained rapid rate in in the 1980s and 1990s, as did Japan in the 1960s; but no country comes close to creating the sheer size and the number of years of high growth rates as China. It makes the Middle Kingdom a good proxy of a large emerging market which is on the verge of maturing. A look at the profit pool of China's largest 200 listed companies as of 2016 also shows a tilt towards three sectors – consumer, industrial and financial. This is exactly in line with the developed markets - an uncanny coincidence. It reaffirms that consumer, industrials and finance sectors inevitably end up constituting a disproportionate share of a market's profit pool as the economy matures.

The only difference between China and the developed markets is the extent of the concentration. In China, more than 85% of its profits came from these three sectors, while it was about two-thirds in the developed economies. The reason for this is the finance sector in China, an outlier contributing excessively to the profit pool. Post-2008 China has pushed its banks and financial institutions to provide more credit to its businesses and people, as well as to foreign countries, in order to fuel its growth rates. The result has been a rapid increase in China's debt position, generating a lot of debate if the economy is excessively indebted, much more than the fundamental ability of those households, businesses or foreign countries to repay. The objective is not to go into a debt-debate, but to assert that the actual contributions of consumer and industrial sectors alone in China is not too different from the developed markets.

Within the BRICS markets, China is the only market that demonstrates this commonality with the developed markets. As of 2016, the bulk of the profit pool in markets like Russia, Brazil and South Africa was still concentrated towards the materials sector, apart from the finance sector. Energy was the third in Russia, while it was utilities in Brazil. In India, the major sectors included technology, apart from finance and energy. For the BRICS group as a whole, the top sectors contributing ~73% of its collective 2016 profit pool were finance, energy and industrial – given China's skewness towards industrial. If one looks at the BRICS ex China grouping only, then the materials sector dominates instead of industrial. In short, these BRICS markets apart from China still have some journey to go before consumer and industrial sectors pick up in prominence.

Turning to the markets of the Bay of Bengal group, is there any hint of the predominant sector in the profit pie of their largest 200 listed companies? Energy and finance continue to be the dominant sectors in the BIMSTEC markets like India, Thailand, Bangladesh and Sri Lanka, with the third being technology in India, industrial in Sri Lanka, materials in Thailand and telecom in Bangladesh. The two markets of the extended Bay of Bengal group, Indonesia and Vietnam, do not conform to this trend. Only finance is common there, not energy. Consumer and telecom are the other two sectors in Indonesia, while it is industrials and materials in Vietnam.

But this is the case of individual markets. What would the picture look like if one looks at this profit pool collectively as a group? What sort of bias does the group portfolio have in the combined profit pie, once the absolute profits are aggregated? In the Bay of Bengal group collectively, the three dominant sectors were financial, energy and technology, as per Bloomberg's data on their 2016 profit numbers. This is because of arithmetic, given the disproportionate size of India's technology sector. The same holds true for the BIMSTEC group alone.

But what is the tilt of the group's other markets excluding India? That would remove the skewness of one disproportionately large member. If India is removed from the Bay of Bengal grouping, then Bay of Bengal ex India has a bias towards financial, energy and consumer. In short, if one removes the disproportionate skewness caused by India's technology sectors, then the remaining markets at least have consumer as the common sector to the experience of China and the developed markets, albeit on an ex India basis for the remaining members' pool. This reaffirms that the remaining markets of this group would give some tilt towards at least one of those sectors (consumer in this case) that is seen to contribute a larger share of the profit pie as markets mature. So while the overall group will have the tilt towards technology due to India's size, combining a portfolio with the Southeast and South Asian markets gives the overall portfolio at least one foot in the door as the two common sectors of consumer and industrials are concerned, at least on an ex India basis. Does this provide an investment rationale to look at this group, considering these two sectors do end up comprising a disproportionate share in markets as they mature and develop further?

A fair mix across manufacturing and services works best

But while this group approach can be an advantage from the perspective of India as it gives the portfolio a tilt towards one of the two magical sectors of consumer and industrial, why would the Southeast Asian markets be interested in a group approach with India? A look at South Korea, one of the poster boys of the emerging markets universe, might offer a possible answer. In South Korea, the three sectors that comprised a disproportionate share of its profit pool in 2016 were consumer, financial and technology. Incidentally, the share of these three sectors was two-thirds of the pie, exactly in line with the developed countries' average. South Korea is pertinent in any discussion of emerging markets because of the sheer investor interest the market has generated. As of February 2017, Bloomberg data showed that approximately 1,300 portfolio funds had over 90% allocation to the South Korean market. This is one of the highest amongst major emerging markets, with the exception of Brazil. Even India, a country with a nominal GDP that is 1.5x that of South Korea has fewer funds allocating 90% to it. Even large emerging markets like Mexico, Russia and Turkey have fewer funds putting 90% allocation to their markets.

One possible answer is in the combination of its sector-exposure, which widens the choices available for investors while allocating their portfolios. South Korea is a unique mix of both manufacturing and services sectors, thanks to its exposure to the consumer and technology spaces. Even China does not enjoy such a mix. If a fair mix across manufacturing and services provide ample choices to investors while giving some reassurance that the mix will cushion the market's performance in case either one sector, manufacturing or services, tanks, then perhaps the increased investor interest to the South Korean market relatively in the emerging markets universe is evidence enough. One assumes this combination of its economic model contributed to make the ship stable and sizable resulting in its promotion to OECD status by 1996, not to mention it gave investors the rationale to make so many funds with an overt allocation to only South Korea.

The same reassurance cannot hold in India or Southeast Asia, since India is overtly exposed to services while the Southeast Asian markets have an excessive bias to manufacturing. A combined Bay of Bengal portfolio can resemble South Korea's composition to some extent, which may augur well for further investor interest. The Bay of Bengal grouping adds India's prowess in the services space due to technology as well as the manufacturing prowess of the Southeast and South Asian markets led by their consumer and industrial sectors (Vietnam and Sri Lanka have a bias towards industrials while Indonesia has a bias towards consumer). This can help the portfolio constituents complement each other to keep the overall portfolio's trajectory upbeat even if any one segment hits headwinds. At the same time, it balances the risk of concentration away from only manufacturing which a singular exposure to the Southeast Asian markets would have done.

Going by the South Korean experience, a fair mix in the portfolio helps evince more interest from investors. Most of them prefer a safer bet in the post-2008 world. Similarly, the complementarity offered within a Bay of Bengal grouping by combining the manufacturing and services sectors augurs well for a portfolio. Those who opine the group's Southeast Asian markets might be better off combining in an ASEAN portfolio should know that a Bay of Bengal grouping does not disturb those markets' tilt towards the consumer sector, rather it only combines them with India's services sector and offers a better balance of the manufacturing and services segments. It also adds mass to the profit base, given the scale of India's corporate sector.

The moot objective here was to show the combination, and what such a combination has evinced elsewhere. If this rationale has no ground, then the investing world should have seen a plethora of ASEAN funds instead of South Korea funds. That has not been the case, has it?

The journey towards concentration is an investment rationale in itself

Our discussion so far has been whether certain sectors end up comprising a disproportionate share of the profits as markets mature. The other question is if the journey towards further concentration can be an investment rationale; and if so, to what extent? How much of the journey is left to traverse? Concentration is inevitable. Countries stress on areas of competitive advantage, and incremental investments flow to feed those sectors, as well as others that complement them. Even talent flows towards those few sectors, going by the choice of courses that new graduates enrol into.

But a relatively diversified profit pool which is still in process of traversing the journey towards concentration offers two opportunities. First, the journey in those dominant sectors is itself an investment journey, because those sectors have to grow further till they end up comprising a more concentrated share of the profit pie. Investing in those growth sectors offers a strong investment rationale, so that investors benefit from the journey left to traverse as the sectors grow and become further concentrated. Of course, this presumes concentration occurs due to profit growth; after all, concentration can occur even in a declining profit scenario. But that is undesirable from the investing perspective. Nevertheless, if a market is highly concentrated, then the journey left to traverse may not offer a reasonable investment rationale. Second, assuming the other contributing sectors are also performing reasonably well in a market with a more diversified profit pool, then it can be an advantage from the perspective of concentration risk. If any market is already too concentrated and its other sectors are not meaningful, the portfolio can face downside risk if a headwind hits those dominant sectors.

If such a market is not yet as concentrated, it may still offer plausible alternatives yet.

Bloomberg profit data of countries offers some clue of their journey left towards concentration. The largest three sectors comprised ~73% of the BRICS collective profit pool in 2016, as compared to the ~51% in the Bay of Bengal group, and ~53% in BIMSTEC alone. Even the ASEAN and SAARC groups had a concentration level in the early-50s. Amongst individual markets, the BRICS markets like Brazil, China and Russia had a concentration level over 85% in 2016. At this rate, how much journey is left in China, Brazil or Russia? If one were to look at the extent of concentration of the top three sectors in those markets' profits, then perhaps they have already traversed that journey. After all, how much higher can one go from 90%? Either the other sectors in these markets are decelerating rapidly, or the dominant sectors are becoming too big. Either way, there is a veritable concentration risk in the equation. In any case, their average concentration is higher than the threshold two-thirds level seen in the case of the developed markets. Neither is the journey that is left long enough, nor do the other sectors offer plausible alternatives, since those sectors have lost their share in a declining profit environment. The arithmetic shows those other sectors have just become too irrelevant.

South Africa is more diversified than Brazil, Russia or China, as its finance sector does not over-dominate its market as it does in the others, which is an irony as Johannesburg houses some of the foremost financial brands of the world. The largest sectors contribute ~70% of the profits in the African country. India is another outlier in the BRICS, with less than ~60% of the profits coming from the largest three sectors. In most cases, these proportions have sustained, or increased, from five years ago in 2011. India is the probable BRICS market that offers an opportunity on both fronts - both in terms of the size of the other sectors it offers and the journey of its dominant sectors that is yet to be traversed.

At the same time, the Bay of Bengal markets had a much lower level of concentration than the BRICS. For instance, Thailand and India had a concentration below 60%, Indonesia and Bangladesh had between 60–70%, while Vietnam and Sri Lanka had a concentration over 70%. These are far less than the ~85% plus levels seen in China, Brazil and Russia.

Given that the threshold average is the two-thirds mark if one goes by the experience of the developed markets, then the journey from the early-50s to the two-thirds mark in the case of the Bay of Bengal group is an investment journey in itself, as their sectors move further towards concentration. On a group basis, the concentration in the Bay of Bengal group as a whole was just ~51% in 2016.

This suggests that the Bay of Bengal portfolio has a longer journey yet to traverse towards concentration, which offers an investment rationale as those sectors gain traction, yet with ample alternatives which still contribute significantly to the overall pie. Moreover, while the share of the top sectors in this group dipped over the last five years between 2012 and 2016 due to the sharp drop in energy sector profits, other sectors continue to show reasonable traction, which is encouraging. As a result, the journey from 51% to two-thirds level gives a hint of the journey towards concentration that is yet to be traversed. In any case, the other sectors are growing which means the duration of the journey towards two-thirds might extend further. That might offer a strong investment rationale to look at this group portfolio.

While the group's overall lower level of concentration is a result of India's numbers (as it contributes a large chunk of the Bay of Bengal group's profit pool), it is important to know that the Bay of Bengal group ex India also had a concentration level of less than 60% from its largest three sectors. Even a sub-60% concentration level is low relative to the developed markets' experience, apart from the other emerging markets.

Do markets really need other sectors?

The other way of looking at this is whether only those few sectors can suffice to meet the economic needs of the nation, or would it demand scaling up of more sectors? Ideally larger countries need more sectors of production, if only to find jobs for its people who possess varying skills which only one or a few sectors cannot entirely accommodate. In a country like Qatar, which may be amongst the richest in the world but is one of the smallest in terms of local population who need to be given jobs, its oil and gas and real estate sectors alone may suffice majorly for that need. In larger nations where the population is in excess of 100 million, not everyone can be employed in just a handful of sectors. Reality demands more sectors, each of which has to be robust enough to go on employing incremental talent as more and more graduates join the workforce each year. From that perspective, a less than 60% concentration ratio in large population countries like India, Thailand and Bangladesh in the Bay of Bengal group is a better deal. Concentration will occur inevitably, but the other sectors also provide reasonable economic opportunity.

In short, the journey towards concentration in this Bay of Bengal group might be a compelling opportunity, whether in the sectors that are yet to grow further or in the other sectors that still comprise a hefty share.

How big is too big? – Is there a tipping point for sectors of competitive advantage?

After looking at sectors that end up comprising a disproportionate share as markets mature, and the journey that is yet to be traversed towards concentration, another question that arises is how big should sectors of competitive advantage be in order to maximise their impact on overall economic growth?

How big is too big, the tipping-point beyond which the sector is no longer maximising its impact on economic growth? After all, a sector of competitive advantage should continue boosting growth significantly. Unfortunately, that does not always happen in the long term. A country starts concentrating its resources disproportionately on only the sectors of competitive advantage, to the extent that the other sectors suffer. This is because the natural progression of market forces may allocate incremental resources towards only those sectors, while ignoring the rest. The other sectors start facing the shortage of good talent, who all want jobs in the coveted larger sectors and study for degrees accordingly. Many of suppliers and financiers start concentrating on only those coveted sectors as they view them as a quicker passage for their own growth, thus limiting the materials and capital the other sectors need to grow. All in all, the other sectors start gasping and their contribution to the economy starts faltering. So while the coveted sectors of competitive advantage continue to grow bigger, its impact on the overall economy starts reducing. Ultimately, this undesirable combination cannot pull the economic ship as it used to. In other words, every rupee of growth in those coveted sectors may effectively yield less and less growth to the overall economy.

Why is this important? To investors, this might give an idea if the broader market is worth investing into or is only that specific sector worth looking at. If one is investing in the market, i.e. the wider range of securities and sectors, then they are essentially investing in the entire economic story. That augurs well for new funds which want to allocate to that market. On the other hand, if one is investing solely in one sector, then only that bit matters; the rest of the economic story is inconsequential. The funds may allocate a small satellite portion to that specific sector, tapering the rationale for more funds dedicated to that broader economy. The Bay of Bengal group is a collection of high-growth economies that are on the verge of seeing traction across multiple sectors. The broader market has to entice an investor in order to earn yield from the economic story. Moreover, an asset class story typically means the economy is the focus, not just singular sector stories. For instance, how many BRICS funds were incepted vs. BRICS materials funds or BRICS technology funds?

From this perspective, if the market is at a stage of evolution where the sector of competitive advantage is no longer maximising its overall impact on economic growth, then it is an undesirable situation. On the other hand, if the sector of competitive advantage is poised to push overall economic growth, then this provides ample investment rationale to look at the economy as a whole, which is desirable.

Looking at the Bloomberg profit data of the listed companies in the specific sectors of competitive advantage in some of the markets under study along with the IMF's WEO data on GDP offers useful insights. The objective was to see how big is too big – if there was a threshold beyond which these sectors start having less and less impact on their country's economic growth. This experiment uses the data of the technology sector in India, textile sector in Bangladesh, materials sector in Brazil, energy sector in Russia and Saudi Arabia, cement sector in Pakistan, consumer discretionary sector in China, food processing sector in Mexico and the electronics sector in South Korea.

The correlation between the YoY growth rates of that sector's profit from 2012 to 2016 and the YoY growth rate of the nominal GDP of that country is first calculated. Thereafter, the ratio of the average profit per company in these sectors of competitive advantage relative to the average profit per company of the largest 200 companies in 2016 is taken. This ratio gives some idea of how big the companies of the sector of competitive advantage were relative to that of the broader market, in terms of their average profit size. Since this experiment is looking at how big a company is becoming, hence average profit was taken rather than aggregate profit. There are obvious limitations, since the listed space may not account for the overall size of an economy. However, this is the data which is publicly available, hence used for country-comparisons.

Over the last five years, the average profit per company in Bangladesh's textile sector grew at a CAGR of 5% as compared to 2% for the overall market. During this period, the relative size of a textile company to an overall company rose from an average 0.1x to 0.2x in 2016. When the YoY growth rates of this sector was matched with the YoY growth rates of the country's GDP, the correlation was approximately 0.3 for these five years. The final numbers to be used are 0.2x for relative size and 0.3 for correlation.

In India, the average profit per company in its technology sector grew at a CAGR of 6% as compared to a 10% de-growth for the overall market. The relative size of a tech company by profits rose from an average 1x to over 2x in this period. Matching the YoY growth of this sector with the YoY growth of India's GDP gives a correlation of approximately 0.8 for these five years. The final numbers to be used are 2x for relative size and 0.8 for correlation.

In China, the average profit per company in its consumer discretionary sector grew at a CAGR of 13% as compared to an 8% growth for the overall market. The relative size of a consumer discretionary company by profits rose from an average 0.4x to 0.5x in this period, and the correlation to its GDP growth was approximately 0.4. The final numbers to be used are 0.5x for relative size and 0.4 for correlation.

In Saudi Arabia, the average profit per company in its energy sector grew at a CAGR of 33% as compared to a 2% de-growth for the overall market. The relative size of an energy company by profits rose from an average 0.2x to 1x in this period. The correlation of this sector's growth with its

GDP growth was approximately 0.8. The final numbers to be used are 1x for relative size and 0.8 for correlation.

In Pakistan, the average profit per company of its cement sector grew at a sheer CAGR of 110% as compared to a 9% growth for the overall market. The relative size of a cement company by profits rose from a mere 0.1x to as much as 2x in this period. The correlation with the GDP was approximately 1.

In South Korea, the average profit per company of its electronics sector grew at a CAGR of 14% as compared to a 2% growth for the overall market. The relative size of an electronics company by profits rose from 3x to 5.5x while the correlation to GDP was a low of 0.04. In Mexico, the average profit per company of its foods sector remained flat in this period, as compared to a 5% de-growth CAGR for the overall market. The relative size of a foods company rose from 1.4x to 1.8x in this period, with a correlation of approximately 0.9.

In Russia, the average profit per company of its energy sector de-grew at a CAGR of 19% as compared to a 14% de-growth for the overall market. The relative size of an energy company by profits declined from 7x to 5x in this period, while the correlation to GDP was a low 0.4. Lastly, Brazil was an outlier because prominent companies in its materials sectors (like Rio Tinto and Vale) saw exceptionally volatile earnings since the last two years in line with global commodity price trends, hence this market is excluded.

Plotting these correlation numbers with the relative size of a company in that sector (as of the closing year) on a graph gives a neat bell-shaped graph. The sweet-spot is the upward-sloping cases where the correlation is on the higher side (say, above 0.5) but the relative size is still below 2x. This denotes the sector is still having a positive, accelerating impact on the overall economic growth, while still retaining some opportunity to grow further relative to the broader market.

Saudi Arabia, Mexico and Pakistan fall in this space in this experiment. India is currently just on the right-side of this sweet-spot, which means that the sector now has lesser impact of its economic growth while growing much larger. The innovations being done in the Indian tech companies currently is a positive in this context. That may see the correlation go up further from current levels, thus shifting it towards the left of the bell-shaped graph. South Korea and Russia lie extreme on the right-side of the graph, which means their sectors of competitive advantage now have a minimal impact on their growth despite growing so large. Bangladesh and China lie on the left-side, which means their sectors are yet to grow big relative to the broader market, and when they do, their impact to the overall economy will grow further. That signifies a good opportunity, since securities in such a situation should ideally be under-valued while carrying healthy prospects.

Bangladesh and India are part of the Bay of Bengal group. Bangladesh is poised to enter the sweet-spot soon, while innovations in India's sector should bring it back in the sweet-spot. This augurs reasonably well from the perspective of looking at this group as an investment proposition.

In conclusion, this chapter looked at whether certain sectors start contributing disproportionately to a market's profit pool as the economy matures, if the journey yet to be traversed in the case of under-concentration offers an investment opportunity in itself, whether the mix of manufacturing and services in a single portfolio offers a rationale, why larger economies still need other sectors to grow and if there is a tipping point beyond which the relative size of the companies in sectors of competitive advantage do not have a maximising impact on the overall economy any more. The findings may not completely offer a tick-mark against the Bay of Bengal group, nonetheless it still offers a reasonably compelling case. As its markets deepen further, the rationale may become more evident, benefiting the investors in that journey.

Long-term Disincentives and Quality Concerns
The Productivity Story

The two segments employing a large chunk of India's overall workforce (skilled and unskilled)

Maid in India is probably as important as Made in India today, in these days of nuclear families with working-couples. Most of these families overtly depend on domestic help to keep their household functioning and take care of the aged, while they go out for their work. The hordes of people migrating to Indian cities for such domestic help jobs are mostly unskilled for any profession. Hence, they resort to domestic help jobs where there are a number of families desperate to hire them without worrying excessively about skills. Most end up earning a good wage without acquiring a proper skill. Satisfaction breeds complacency, and that further reduces the incentive to skill. At the same time, hordes of people with skills working in Indian cities face a salary crunch. With many businesses under continued profit pressure and hyper-competition for jobs, salary growth has not grown for many. Survival breeds unaffordability, and reduces the ability to skill further. Most of these businesses fall under the small enterprise categories, not the sunrise sectors like technology, retail or finance where most of the high-salary growth has been concentrated. They employ a large chunk of India's skilled population.

A visit to a friend's home in Gurgaon in 2016 also helped highlight the dichotomy between these two groups. His is a family of five, including his parents and child. His spouse also works. They are home only for a few hours in the night. Thus, hiring a full-time domestic help is inevitable. Their domestic help is from the Indian province of West Bengal. This person's boarding, lodging, doctor's fee in case of illness and a ticket for his annual holiday to his village are all borne by my friend as an incentive to make him stay. When skirmishes between Bengal's two political parties cause damage to this person's village, my friend helps with funds to rebuild his home. He is unskilled for any profession, yet has seen his monthly salary grow from Rs. 8000 to Rs. 12,000 in three years. It is all tax-free, apart from all these perks and a stay-at-home job. My friend's neighbour is a family from the Indian province of Uttar Pradesh. Their daughter is college-educated, speaks English and works in one of the many call-centres in Gurgaon. She is skilled for her profession, yet earns a monthly salary of Rs. 16,000 before tax, without any perks and wasting hours daily in traffic-jams. It is her cost to pay for doctors, any calamity to her home or vacations. Her salary has not grown much in the last few years, and it is enough she has a job because cost-cutting is rampant.

Both these groups mentioned above comprise a large proportion of India's working-age population. Such examples abound. On one hand, a dependency on domestics who know they are indispensable; on the other, a glut in salary growth in process-driven and small enterprise jobs which employ a significant number of people. The salary earned being unskilled does not seem too different from the salary earned in process-jobs like tele-calling or customer service or as skilled workers in small enterprises. Education and skilling may be the route to a prosperous life, but the dynamics of demand and supply is creating a growing disincentive and inability to skill. Given this situation, the question is whether the growing disincentive or inability of a large chunk of India's working-age to skill is impacting the productivity of the country in the long term? While it may be debatable to brand this situation as a disincentive or inability to skill, it still questions the future of India's productivity!

The two segments employing a large chunk of India's skilled workforce

While giving a talk in Kuala Lumpur in 2017, our discussion went on to the future of work (i.e. skilled work). My opinion, based on seeing the developments in India, was that the work of the future would grow mainly in two segments – one is the high-level ideation to develop new innova-tions and breakthroughs which will demand the best-of-the-best brains;

the other is of low-paid process-driven services jobs that are execution-oriented.

This is because the heightened need to maintain a competitive edge and grow in a hyper-competitive business environment will drive the need for innovations and cost-maintenance; hence these two segments. The first segment will need a smaller number of people, while the second segment will need many more people.

The second segment faces a challenge

The second segment here is common to the second group mentioned in the example earlier in this chapter. Time will tell whether the work of the future will indeed turn out like this. If it does, the existent salary trends may play a spoiler for ensuring an adequate long term supply of productive workers in this second segment.

Consider the arithmetic. In the example of Gurgaon, the domestic help's Rs. 12,000 wage is a princely sum given the low cost of living in the village where his family stays and spends this income, and his income has only grown. His expenses to prepare for this job were nil, so the return is literally manifold. Conversely, his neighbour's Rs. 16,000 salary is a pittance given the cost of living in Gurgaon where she stays and spends this income, and the income has not grown much. Her expenses to prepare for her job were far higher as are her day-to-day living expenses, so the return seems ludicrous.

Place this at an aggregate level for the country, and one has a situation where many workers across India are now looking at these two cases and are questioning if they would indeed earn better returns by investing in any major skill. Skilling does not seem to show the disproportionate returns as one would have hoped, at least in this segment of process-driven jobs which employ a large portion of India's youth today.

Incidentally, many of them may not opt to do domestic jobs as it seems demeaning to them. That is even worse, because that would mean they are both unskilled and unproductive. How will the country be productive in such a situation?

One can argue these examples are circumstantial and so inferences may be misleading; but there is a large gap between population and employable population in India. If one adds this challenge of a growing disincentive or inability to skill, then the country is headed towards tricky waters in the long term. This is probably as big a challenge as the challenge of job-creation itself. Unproductivity would only delay income growth and realizing the demographic dividend. As this gap between ability and aspiration becomes endemic, it can hit social stability. Perhaps it is all the more imperative that youth is educated about the real incentives to skill, else the irrational perceptions of some of them might threaten the region's demographic dividend in the long term.

The first segment faces a challenge too

While workers in the process-driven jobs may face a growing disincentive to skill due to low and flat salaries, even the ideation/innovation jobs face a challenge. This is to do with the quantity and quality of education. As per India's Ministry of Human Resources Development (MHRD) report, the number of universities in India grew from 621 to about 800 over the five years till 2015–2016, a CAGR of only 5%. Much of this incremental growth has been concentrated in only a few provinces (i.e. Uttar Pradesh, Gujarat, Rajasthan, Uttarakhand and Assam). So the incremental spread is concentrated in specific areas, a concern for the rest of the country from the perspective of improved access to university education.

However, India's gross enrolment ratio for higher education is still low at 24.5% as of 2015–16, as per the MHRD report. Within this, the university student enrolment as a proportion to the population in the age group of 18 to 23 years is even lower. Of course, university enrolment does not include the industrial and skill training institutes, an area where the current Indian government's National Skill Development programme has made significant inroads, but a lot still remains to be done. Anyway, the eventual supply of qualified talent needed to feed the country's expected growth might fall short of the demand in jobs that need degrees. Any supply shortage will only drive up the price of talent – good for employees but bad for investors. It may even necessitate import of talent into a large population country.

94

Let us come to my personal experience. While giving guest lectures to students across universities in India, Sri Lanka, Bangladesh, Vietnam, Indonesia and Thailand, there seemed a discernible gap in the quality of most of the students from the perspective of their critical and analytical thinking abilities when situational questions were asked. Many of these universities had good ranks in the ranking tables. Of course, there were exceptions. But the average was on the lower side. Situational questions have always been part of my agenda during talks, so the interaction with students also moves along that line. Their answers for such situational questions told me a lot about the quality of thinking in the students in these top-ranked universities. It seemed most are good in mugging up formulae and theories and vomiting it out in exams, rather than in critical and analytical thinking. Perhaps course curriculums are set on those lines, but if this talent has to be developed for innovative and ideation, then the talent quality may play a spoiler for ensuring an adequate supply of productive workers in the first segment, i.e. the innovative and ideation oriented jobs.

This shortage can create an additional issue. The few shining stars would know their worth very well. That may drive greed to maximise their monetisation, resulting in frequent churning in their employment. Companies would be willing to shell out; who else will they turn to for thinking the new innovations and breakthroughs? This is a downside risk for business profits, and a challenge for investors. If the higher incremental cost of these stars comes out from what is paid to the process-driven workers, it would put even more pressure on that second segment, which would only exacerbate their disincentive to skill and hit their productivity.

So far, the narrative has concentrated, from the Indian context, on the productivity challenges the workforce might face in the long term. All is not doom; indeed if the country incentivizes and educates the youth to skill and improves the quality of higher education towards critical and analytical thinking, then the long term supply of productive workforce in both the segments can stay intact. Let us now turn to recent history.

Recent history bears good news on productivity

Incremental output of a country can be measured as an increase in the productivity of its workforce along with an increase in its workforce. As per the data from the International Labour Organisation (ILO) on country-wise labour productivity (ILO modelled estimates), the maximum growth in productivity since the last five years till 2016 took place in China, which saw a 7% CAGR in output per worker. The fact that the most populous country also demonstrated the maximum improvement in productivity should be food for thought for all nations with large population. This was followed by Cambodia, Myanmar, Sri Lanka, Ethiopia and Ireland with a 6% CAGR each. Two of them are part of the Bay of Bengal group. Next in line were India and Laos with a 5% CAGR each, followed by Vietnam, Bangladesh, Tanzania, Rwanda and the Philippines with a 4% CAGR each and Thailand, Indonesia, Bhutan, Romania and the UAE with a 3% CAGR each. Six of them are part of the Bay of Bengal group. The rest of the world lags with a 2% CAGR, or even less. BRICS countries like Russia, Brazil and South Africa were close to nil, and even a −1% in Brazil's case.

Every data has its own shortcoming. Nevertheless, if one has to take an approximate indication from publicly available data, then the point of listing the nations by productivity improvement is to highlight that eight of the Bay of Bengal group countries demonstrated a fair improvement in recent history – one of the few groups of developing countries to do so. Even ASEAN or BRICS do not have so many of their members amongst these top-performers. It also highlights that large population countries can amply improve productivity to increase their output. Some of the top ranked countries have a sizable population, like Indonesia, Ethiopia, China, India and Bangladesh. If productivity improvement is under focus, then it is positive from the investing perspective.

Turning to the expectations till 2021, the good news extends here as well. Again, data projection has its own limitations; but investors looking at a horizon of the next few years should note this indicatively. As per the ILO's data on labour productivity, the maximum growth in productivity expected from now till 2021 will be in Bhutan at 7% CAGR. China, India and Myanmar are expected to follow with a 6% CAGR. Bangladesh, Sri Lanka, Vietnam, Cambodia, Laos and the Philippines are next with a 5% CAGR each, followed by Ethiopia and Indonesia with a 4% CAGR each. Thailand, Pakistan and Iran come next with a 3% CAGR each. This includes eight of the Bay of Bengal markets. The uptick in productivity should continue here for some years.

Apart from the fact that most of the Bay of Bengal group countries are expected to improve productivity, it is pertinent to note that most of the other countries that improved their productivity in the last five years are also expected to continue doing so. Productivity improvements seem to be very scarcely spread indeed.

Both productivity and workforce addition should contribute to incremental national output

But in large population countries, just looking at productivity will be incomplete. They also need to increase their labour workforce so that more and more graduates and skilled personnel can find good jobs. Job creation is important to maintain social stability in countries with large populations. Job creation in turn also impacts productivity. This is because as more and more people enter the job-field and start competing with each other, it creates a natural incentive for people to push their productivity so that they stay ahead of the curve and grow better than the rest. So while the chapter is about the productivity part of national output creation, it needs to look at the workforce part of national output too.

Assuming the contribution of productivity and workforce towards incremental output to be typically 50:50 in large population countries, then a comparison of the CAGR in productivity (output per worker) with the CAGR in GDP may be interesting. Of course, the contribution should ideally be calculated on an absolute basis, instead of incrementally on the growth rates. Due to the paucity of publicly available data across countries, this experiment makes use of only growth rates. Using the ILO's data on labour productivity and the IMF's WEO data, all those countries that showed a positive growth in both metrics are taken. The objective is to see how much the first metric contributed towards the second, i.e. whether the growth rate in productivity was approximately 0.5x of the growth rate in national output? Or was it closer to nil or closer to 1x, at either extreme.

For the last five years till 2016, this contribution was between 0.4x to 0.6x (average 0.5x) for Bangladesh, Nepal, Vietnam, Cambodia, Laos, South Korea, Pakistan and Tanzania. They are ideally placed in terms of incremental contribution from both productivity and job-creation. Three of them are part of the Bay of Bengal group.

As many as six of the group countries, including India, Thailand, Indonesia, Sri Lanka, Myanmar and Bhutan, saw a higher than 0.6x contribution of productivity towards national output. This indicates job-growth is not happening much and they need to ramp up their workforce significantly – a negative from the perspective of widening the consumption stories of these countries. Not enough people are getting jobs, and resulting incomes.

For the next few years till 2021, this contribution is expected to be between 0.4x to 0.6x for Indonesia, India, Thailand, Bangladesh, Bhutan, Myanmar, Vietnam, Poland, Ethiopia, Romania, Egypt, South Korea and the Philippines. As many as seven of them are part of the Bay of Bengal group, which augurs well from the expectation of job-growth and productivity contribution. The long term productivity challenges discussed at the beginning of this chapter may not show colour till 2021, but still remain pertinent from the longer-term perspective. Sri Lanka is the only exception from this group which is expected to see a higher share of its output coming from productivity improvement rather than from labour growth. Nevertheless, investors looking at a horizon till 2021 can take solace that the workforce and productivity situations in most of the countries in this group are largely expected to remain stable in this period.

Even China is expected to see a higher incremental contribution from productivity rather than workforce addition in the coming years till 2021, just like Sri Lanka. That is a concern in a large population country. The imperative to push labour employment is probably one reason for its thrust to the Belt and Road Initiative since its projects employ a large number of Chinese labourers and engineers in overseas projects. This reduces the dependence on local employment to absorb this workforce. During a trip to Colombo in 2017, few Chinese labourers sat waiting with me at the bus-stop in Kollupitiya at 5 a.m. They dropped off at the Port City site near the Fort area, a reclamation project being developed by the Chinese. Ideally, one would want that countries with a large population to demonstrate an increase in both labour force and productivity. The good news is that at least in the near-term, the data of most of the Bay of Bengal group countries shows they are well placed on both fronts.

Where were the BRIC countries back in 2001? That might make an inter-esting comparison. In the year 2000–2001, only Russia, China and India had shown a positive growth in productivity improvement, ranging from 2% in India to 5% in Russia and 8% in China. China has maintained a high growth in productivity since that time, which is noteworthy. Brazil saw a drop in productivity that year. In terms of the contribution of productivity towards national output, it was half only in India. This contribution was higher in China, which means it faced a disproportionate pressure on its labour participation even then, just like it is expected to do in 2021.

Real assets face a productivity challenge too

Another data may be useful here. ROE of a company is the ratio of perfor-mance of a company. Its formula can be broken up as per the Du-Pont method, into profitability (profit per revenue earned), productivity (revenue earned per assets employed) and leverage (assets employed per equity invested). As per the Bloomberg data for the largest 200 listed companies by 2016 market capitalisation across two-dozen key devel-oping markets, the productivity component declined between 2021 and 2016 collectively in several emerging markets like South Korea, Mexico, India, China, Turkey, Russia, Brazil, Thailand and the Philippines. Of course, this ratio includes all the resources used by a business, not just the work-force. Hence, if one correlates this Bloomberg data with the ILO data shown previously, one can conclude that productivity of the non-work-force resources has reduced appreciably in markets like India, Thailand, China and the Philippines; this is because they showed labour productivity improvement coupled with a resources productivity decline for this period.

This mean that their real assets like land and buildings and intangible assets like technology are not being used productively, or there is over-capacity in the system. Given that the investment rate is expected to pick up or remain high in some of these countries, improving the productivity from resources is all the more imperative.

Is the hunger for gaining new skills missing

So the near-term bears good news as far as productivity and workforce participation of this group's countries is concerned, despite some challenges to drive productivity, skilling and learning in the long term. However, skills, incentive and motivation aside, the youth also have to have the hunger to skill and succeed. With many rural youth enjoying the monetary comforts from the sale of their ancestral farm land for infrastructure projects, the ease of new money has retarded the hunger for gaining new knowledge and doing productive work. Many of these youth are not willing to do the work their parents did (like farming) because they do not view it at a par with their new status, nor have they acquired any new skill or knowledge to do anything on their own steam. At the same time, the consumerism culture that accompanies new money is driving down the probability of saving from this windfall. This is an attitude problem that is impacting the economic hunger of a section of the young, working-age population from gaining new knowledge and doing productive work, while creating a potential gap between ability and aspiration. How does a country of India's population cope with this? Becoming productive presupposes the workforce is participating in the first place. If that is not happening adequately, then any talk on productivity will only be half addressed. Should the government introduce incentives that push this newly-moneyed class to use financial windfalls towards further education or skilling, rather than frenzied consumerism?

As it is, there are enough threats. From driverless trains to virtual banking, technology is all pervasive. The degree of automation and robotics in developing countries may be less than in the developed countries, it is a real threat for jobs nevertheless – especially for those who do not have the ability or cannot afford to learn new skills.

In conclusion, this chapter took a look at the broader issues affecting the long term productivity of specific sections of the workforce, especially those that make up a large chunk in India. There is a growing inability and disincentive to skill in some segments and workers have to be educated to see the benefits of skilling. It raises two challenges that may impact the long term supply of productive employees: a growing disincentive to skill and a shortage of critical thinking. At the same time, the near-term outlook on productivity improvement in most of the Bay of Bengal countries remains healthy and they are expected to see both productivity and work-force addition contribute to incremental output.

To add a postscript here: Possessing English language skill is a colonial legacy in India, and is often considered as a yardstick for competence, education and getting interview-calls. Indians view English skills with the same fervour as they view acquiring other knowledge and skills. Is it a necessity? Yes, offshored jobs from the West may need this skill, but it is not a necessity to get ahead in every corporate race. During my interactions in Indonesia, Thailand and Vietnam, it turned out most of their corporate professionals speak and write limited English, some none at all. Yet some of these countries have seen high interest from foreign businesses setting up shop since the 1980s. Their business sectors were expansive, when India's was yet to open up. The number of foreign brands in their malls or roads is more than those seen in India even today. Foreigners have happily done business in these countries for several decades without a majority of the locals possessing English skills, despite much of the business interest coming from Anglo-speaking countries like Britain, the USA or Australia. Their locals rode their countries' growth journey without good English skills. Yes, knowing the language always helps, but it is not as critical as it is made out to be. Perhaps Indians should instead concentrate those efforts to push other knowledge and skills to its youth, so that they become a more productive workforce in the long term.

The PTP Model and Implications
The Formalisation Story

Of all the things Indians have successfully copied from other countries, the "ojek" is probably one of the best things they never copied. Born in Brazil, ojek is a motorcycle taxi that has become very popular across most of the Southeast Asian countries over the last two decades. Why? First, in cities which are notoriously traffic-jam prone, it does not fall prey to miles long bumper-to-bumper traffic jams like cars do. That means one reaches destinations fast and time is not wasted unproductively. Second, in cities where the cost of living including public commute has been rising, it is one of the cheapest forms of transport one can use without embracing the human-rush in buses and urban commuter trains. Third, in cities where taxis are becoming increasingly hard to get and app-based cabs can mean spiked fares if demand is high, an ojek is available conveniently at every street corner or in very quick time on the app, all at a standardised price.

Little wonder that the ojek has become so popular across Southeast Asia. In South Asian cities like Mumbai, Bengaluru, Delhi, Kolkata, Kathmandu or Dhaka which are equally traffic-prone, expensive and running-taxis are hard to find, it is a wonder why this convenient mode of transport is non-existent. Maybe the South Asia people prefer a four-wheeled car as a show of ostentatious lifestyle. Or maybe they are wary of the lack of lane-driving in their countries. Or perhaps the government is resistant in allowing this business due to the taxi-lobby, but that is fodder for another discussion. The objective here is to look at the ojeks of Southeast Asian countries, some of which are part of the Bay of Bengal group. Whilst travelling in various cities in Indonesia, Vietnam and Cambodia on these ojeks, both the traditional ones and the app-based ones, it was interesting to chat with the drivers and see how technology had compelled formalisation, thus widening the business from what it was a few years ago.

The PTP Model, and examples from the Bay of Bengal markets

A good way of looking at formalisation is through what is termed as the PTP Model in this book. PTP refers to Process, Technology and Policy, the catalysts through which the movement towards formalisation is occurring in many countries. Sometimes changes in the processes of a business were the trigger. Technology is a big catalyst towards formalisation across businesses. Neither process nor technology innovations alone can scale up the movement; it also needs policy to help it scale it up in a big way. Hence, the PTP Model! Below are some examples from the Bay of Bengal group countries that demonstrate this push towards formalisation.

The ojek mobile apps that have become very popular in Southeast Asia include Gojek and Grab, amongst others. The ojek drivers in Indonesia, Vietnam and Cambodia told me that driving an ojek had become one of the easiest sources of income for any semi-educated or uneducated person over the last few years. Bikes were often shared instead of owned, and procuring a bike was not too expensive. Most operators did not even need registration as taxis. There were ojeks working only part-time when they were free to work or were returning from their normal activities; for instance, an ojek driver who once gave me a ride in Phnom Penh was a family-man returning home after dropping his boy to school. The issue was – the business itself was run on a totally informal manner, often resulting in arguments over prices and routes.

Now thanks to technology, the system became more formal with the entry of the motorcycle taxi apps. The mobile app companies demand that the bikes should have proper registration, uniforms are worn, driving licenses are checked and the ownership proved before any driver can be empaneled by the mobile app company. Allotting of routes to the nearest bike is done transparently as per location on the app. Ratings give incentives, compelling drivers to improve their communication and customer behaviour. All these have been possible due to technology, which has helped transform the entire ojek culture, both for drivers and passengers.

Many people who earlier avoided the traditional ojeks due to the haggling over prices and routes have now migrated to using the app-based ojeks, thus widening the business in the country with more drivers and passengers. Clients prefer the convenience of an app-based ojek ride, to the extent that even girls in fashionable attire often use them in Jakarta, something that would be unheard of in many other cities. Exact data is not available, but Gojek is estimated to have over 300,000 drivers across Indonesia while Grab is estimated to have over 75,000 drivers across Southeast Asia. This formalisation helped all these drivers enter the virtuous cycle of incomes and jobs.

Yes, there is still the odd case of an app-based ojek not turning up or a passenger having to wait long till the driver turns up. Also, every app-based ojek driver may not be as skilled as a traditional ojek driver, because many app-based drivers are new drivers while most traditional drivers have plied their trade for years. That can eventually impact the ride's duration. For instance, while squeezing through a tight jam in Jakarta's Kalibata area, my traditional ojek driver skilfully navigated through the gridlock while many app-based ojek drivers struggled. Nevertheless, the app-based ojeks are pushing formalisation of this business. The adoption may be fast or slow, but it is occurring. This trend towards adoption of new technologies augurs well for the formalisation of many sectors across the countries of the Bay of Bengal group, especially in those sectors hitherto thought chronically informal. That itself opens up a plethora of new investment avenues. All in all, the app-based ojeks of Southeast Asia is a useful example of how technology helps the formalisation of a business – the T in the PTP Model.

This formalisation through technology is not only creating measurable incomes and a structured way of doing the business, but it is also opening up new avenues. In India's e-commerce space, the players have helped aggregate hundreds and thousands of fragmented sellers from across the huge country on a formal platform. Due to this, the exact flow of business of each seller can now be measured, the closest substitute one can have to a proper audit. This has created the opportunity to give them working capital loans on their sales, which helps them scale up further. This source of funding was not possible earlier when the business was flowing in an unorganized manner, and is an example of how technology-led formalisation opens up new avenues.

Another example of technology-led formalisation comes from Bangladesh's microfinance industry, as seen during my trip in 2005 to do an internship with Grameen Bank, the global microfinance major. This was before modern-day mobile apps came into vogue. Back in those days, the ubiquitous public calling-telephone was the common norm in Indian cities for communicating while on-the-go. The problem in Bangladesh, and similar poor countries, was the investments needed to lay the wiring for such landline telephony. Hence, Grameen Bank started the Village Phone ladies concept. Under this, the woman borrower was given the loan to buy a mobile phone and run it as a public calling phone in her village. A wireless mobile was more economical to set up, as it did not need wiring till the door-step. This created a more organized method of public communication which was available close at hand, made possible by technology; unlike earlier when instant communication on-the-go for the locals was possible only by using one's connections with the few elite who had mobiles or walking a long way to the nearest public call landline. It may not be an exact definition of the modern-day technology-led formalisation of business, but they did help create a more organized and deeper penetrated business in those days in Bangladesh, one of the Bay of Bengal group countries.

Turning to Process, the P in the PTP Model, an example exists in Grameen Bank itself. Local money lenders were traditionally the main source of finance in the villages. The system was unorganised, their rate of interest used to be prohibitive, and the debt often became an albatross around the neck running into generations of the borrower's family. Grameen Bank put in place the self-help group process as a social alternative to material collateral, which the poor families anyway lacked. Apart from the self-help group process, the Bank put in place other operating processes to ensure asset quality and recovery, while facilitating the distribution of credit for entrepreneurial activities across Bangladeshi village women. Visits to several branches and homes in those villages gave me ample anecdotes of how this process has helped the families, and the business itself. As a result, organised microfinance picked up across the districts, and the incomes helped uplift the social quality of life of millions of rural families. It is no wonder that Bangladesh has improved on many social indicators to become one of the best in the South Asian region, even ahead of its larger neighbour India on many counts. Women, who were a marginalized section relegated to informal funding, have become mainstream economic bread-winners, thanks to a formalized funding industry. Their repayment habits became a yardstick for further loans, akin to credit scores, thus helping them enter the formal cycle of saving, investing and borrowing. They had to open bank accounts, and had to sign their names using a signature instead of thumb-print while taking the loan. This ability of writing opened many women to further formal business activities. This is a type of process improvement, which acted as a catalyst towards formalisation.

In India, the Self Employed Women's Association (SEWA) is an example of organizing women workers through formalized processes to negotiate terms. Provision of official certificates through designated skill-service providers, as is now happening in Nepal and India, is another process that can help informal workers enter the formal work sector. Formalisation in tourism is an area where Southeast Asia stands out relative to South Asia, with organised service-providers making it convenient and safe to travel. These are just some of the examples of process-led formalisation of businesses.

But no change can be scaled up at a mass-level unless Policy backs it up – the other P in the PTP Model. Several retail banks in India launched mobile apps and were trying to migrate customers from branches to apps on the premise that the app was more economical and convenient for most banking needs, but the migration towards digital banking received its biggest push after the government's demonetisation policy in 2016. More people started using digital banking apps after this announcement than they did before.

Policy also extends to working-conditions of a business. During my first trip to Dhaka in 2005, my guest-house was in a working-class neighbourhood called Shyamoli. The area was crowded because several informal factories were housed in the dilapidated buildings around there. A tragic disaster in a major garment factory in Savar in 2013 forced its government to work on policies for worker safety and building compliances. During my next trip to Dhaka in 2017, curiosity made me revisit that neighbourhood to see if improvements had really been done to the small factories in Shyamoli. Yes, the buildings looked much sturdier than before, due to the repairs that had been effected. This is an example of policy bringing in some formal changes in a sector.

But policy changes can negatively impact a business too, despite the right intentions. In such situations, stakeholders need a further push to ensure their willingness to adapt or their ability to adapt. For instance, the GST Tax policy implemented in India in 2017 was a step to create a uniform taxation system across all the provinces of India, as compared to the earlier confusing system wherein each province had its own tax rates leading to opportunities for slippage in tax tracking and compliance. However, several small-businesses have struggled to implement the new rules, especially as the initial cost of higher compliance hit them hard financially. In such situations, policy should also ensure that some of the incremental taxation income coming from the policy pushing an organised system like GST is used partly to give incentives to small businesses to adapt to the new rules. Building education and awareness of the new compliances is an important capacity-building step that policy needs to include, so that the lack of comprehension is not an impediment to adapt to the newer, organised system. The RERA Act in India was a policy to make its murky and unorganized real estate sector cleaner and organized. The intent was correct; but many players deliberately slowed down their real estate projects till they could find new loopholes to exploit. So policy has to ensure that deliberate miscreants are black-listed. That would force the willingness to adapt instead of resorting to the old ways, and avoid negative fallouts like businesses deliberately going slow under specific circumstances.

At the same time, policy may be unable to formalize the entire value-chain every time. Many businesses are becoming formal, but many of their suppliers remain informal. The automobile sector is an example, where many spare-part making companies still employ informal workers in unorganized set-ups. That gives them a cost-advantage, which translates into a lower price for the end car. Policy can formalize the primary sector, but it may not always be able to drill down to formalize the rest of the value-chain. While some of these primary businesses may prefer suppliers only from the organized, formal sector, not everyone may show such moral responsibility. In short, some amount of informality may always co-exist with the formal.

Nevertheless, policy is an important catalyst, and many of the Bay of Bengal group countries continue to make progress on this front. In terms of organising the labour market itself, Nepal is in the process of drafting employee and labour policies for the informal sector. Similarly, Bangladesh is exploring formal identity cards and worker insurances to its construction workers. India is institutionalizing formal training programmes in labour laws for workers and is studying a voluntary code of conduct on contractual labour. With three-fourths of the global informal employment concentrated in India, Pakistan, Mexico, Brazil, Vietnam and the Philippines, two of which are part of the Bay of Bengal group, the need for driving policy action to organise the labour market is an imperative, not just organising the business sectors.

With the Bay of Bengal economies poised to see a reasonable rate of growth over the next few years till 2021, one hopes it would enhance their ability to push further policy towards formalisation of businesses, so that the business sectors become further penetrated and offer a wider opportunity to investors.

Formalisation has implications for businesses and investors

First, formalisation typically leads to some industry consolidation, which means few large players controlling a majority of the market share and the growing irrelevance of the smaller, marginalized players. One reason for such consolidation is that the cost of doing business goes up due to new rules. Many small businesses across countries like India are viable only because they are unorganized, and do not have to bear compliance costs. If they had to, they would not be viable anymore. Let alone viability, there is an added incentive to remain small because the government starts taxing businesses only beyond a certain size. This is one of the reasons why most of the business sectors across South Asia continue to be dominated by micro/small enterprises. Formalisation necessitates compliance, and many cannot bear the new cost. So they either sell out or shut down, and the market share becomes concentrated with a few big players.

From the investing perspective, many global investors have to comply with a minimum size criterion when selecting investments, and so the creation of larger, though fewer, companies as a result of consolidation is an advantage as it expands the pool they are willing to look at. Investors need to take this into account, specifically in the Bay of Bengal markets like Bangladesh and Sri Lanka where the average size of a company is smaller.

The companies benefiting from formalisation there might offer a compelling investment opportunity as they scale up further, and reach the minimal size required by those investors.

Second, creation of a few large companies has ramifications for urbanisation, and all the services associated with urbanisation like housing, transport, retail, etc. Since only a few large companies scale up, they can employ a larger workforce than the others. That will drive urbanisation towards those clusters which house these few large firms. The global average rate of urbanisation is 50%. The Bay of Bengal group countries like India, Bangladesh, Vietnam and Myanmar have a lower rate of urbanisation at 30–35%, with Sri Lanka and Nepal ranking even lower. This journey from 30% to 50% might accelerate in the coming years, but more importantly, it may accelerate more in the few urban clusters where the larger companies benefiting from formalisation-led consolidation are based. Hence, the services businesses also have to target those towns.

From the investing perspective, investors have to target those services (housing, transport, retail, etc.) that are looking to expand in only those urban clusters; because that is where the primary opportunity will expand.

Third, such consolidation can change the nature of competition in that business, which can compress margins and pricing power. When an industry is fragmented, buyers and sellers may not always know what the market is doing in terms of the pricing and the willingness to pay. When the competitive intensity is concentrated around only a few large businesses, there is transparency of who is charging what. That can trigger a price war to win market share. For instance, India's telecom sector is an example of consolidation-induced price wars. Self-constructed homes may be a better example. Typically, the construction of a self-constructed house was based on B2C relationships with an informal lot of suppliers and contractors. After RERA and other policies help drive some formalisation into the real estate sector, it may create a few large builders who are compliant as per the rules. That may create a bidding war amongst those few large builders since the client has to deal with only those few. Whether that can occur in the self-construction segment is something one has to wait and see, because large builders might not even have an incentive to look at individual houses. Nevertheless, such scenarios can put pressure on margins and the pricing power.

From the investing perspective, the key becomes to track the businesses in that sector that have the capacity to win volumes, since not all will have adequate capacity. Since money (profits) cannot always be won on the price-factor anymore, the volume-factor becomes the next important metric for investors to track which businesses will ultimately make some money in that industry. A volume-driven business also means more demand for the raw materials, and so the volume-formula extends further down to those suppliers too.

Fourth, it may keep up the tempo on offshoring and production migration, something that could benefit the Bay of Bengal countries. Some services are being outsourced from the Western countries to India and Sri Lanka, while some manufacturing is being outsourced from China to Bangladesh and Vietnam. The next stage of offshoring will also extend to regional value-chains and near-shoring. Many products manufactured in China source a large portion of their value chain from the regional markets. Firms within the Bay of Bengal group that deal in those segments need to be proactive to win this business away from the other Asia Pacific countries. If they do not have the capacity, it is an incentive for them to invest in it. If production migrates from China to Vietnam or Bangladesh, the group countries should try to capture the entire value-chain within the group's countries. Near-shoring can be the next level of services outsourcing. Most services offshored to India come from the West. Even countries like Japan, Taiwan and Singapore may now look to outsource services in order to save on costs and substitute their lack of a young working-age population. Some countries in the Bay of Bengal group are ideally placed to capture this flow, due to cost, talent and time-zone benefits.

From the investing perspective, such regional value-chains, near-shoring and production migration can open up a whole host of investible companies to look at in the Bay of Bengal markets, especially those that have the capacity and are able to organize their operations to be eligible to compete for those business flows.

Fifth, a more competitive business environment due to formalisation will also means changes for employees. It means an on-going demand to skill and re-skill. The cost of preparing for a job may go up, but it will also drive productivity in those businesses. That is good for the growth of business, employees and investors in the long-run. It may not be possible for every person to reskill all the time, be it for costs, logistics or family concerns; hence there can be a harsh cost on people due to formalisation. At the same time, cost pressures of formalisation may necessitate the demand for more contractual workers as they may be cheaper than regular employees. As per an ILO report on Indian labour participation, the share of organized wage/salary workers in India's workforce reduced from 18% in 2015 to 15% in 2016. This 85% share of the unorganized sector crosses 90% if one adds informal workers of the formal sector, most of whom are contractual and casual. As per the India-KLEMS database, employment in India grew by a mere 1.2% between 2001 and 2011, far less than its GDP. So not only is India's employment growth minimal, an increasing portion is going to contractual and casual labour. Contractual labour might negate the benefits employees expect to earn following formalisation of the business, in case the benefits provided to an organized workforce need not be paid to a contractual workforce.

From the investing perspective, businesses that can bring down the cost of workforce with contractual workers may be attractive since they have a better chance to improve profitability. The challenge will be if any break in the continuity of quality talent hits the firm's product quality, since that can lead to client attrition. Also, any break in the income of a contractual worker can hit his continuity as an addressable consumer. Contractual labour can impact the demand for some businesses that depend on a regular flow of income, say loans. Personal credit assessment is a standard process for regular employees who get a salary every month. Contractual workers might face the same challenges as self-business people, since the tenure of their income ends with their contract. The loan repayment can be fitted within that contract period, but that may not always be feasible in long-duration larger loans. At the same time, formalisation can help widen the base of addressable consumers. The microfinance borrowers are an example.

Entrepreneur support has to accompany formalisation

So what about employees who lose out in the race towards formalisation, since not everyone has resources to re-skill? Or those hopefuls who were looking to enter the job-front, but cost pressures have reduced hiring. Businesses may not step up to provide skilling facilities, if saving profit margins is the primary concern. In large population countries, this can become a socio-political issue. New ways to economically engage such employees have to be thought of. Entrepreneurship has to be further institutionalized through mentorship and funding support, as an alternative means to job creation. Microfinance is an example, which has already created entrepreneurial avenues for several thousand people across countries. Social business as a concept is also picking up in the Bay of Bengal region to connect entrepreneurship ideas with the critical development challenges of this region. The Yunus Centre in Bangladesh has instituted a periodic social business forum inviting business ideas to solve development challenges; the businesses then receive funding support. Such entrepreneurs may end up creating the next generation of businesses to invest in this region, something investors need to take note of.

The two-step process towards organised/ formalised business

In order to compare the degree of organized sector in the economy, an assumption of the two-step process towards organised/formalised business may be interesting to investigate. Listed companies data has been taken in most of the analysis in this book since that is publicly available. Assuming the sales (revenues) of the largest listed companies to be a proxy for the economic output created by the broader business sector, then the ratio of corporate revenue to GDP gives a possible measure of the proportion of the organized sector to its total economic output (real economy). This becomes a two-step process towards formalisation because the listed space is not a complete representation of its business sectors. So the first-step of formalisation is the process to formalise all the business-sectors in the real economy, and the second-step is to list all those big businesses.

This is an inadequate method to compare the degree of organized sector in the economy, but the idea is to conduct a cross-country comparison of how large the organised, listed space is. From the perspective of investing, more good businesses should be listed so that they can be invested into. A small proportion of the listed space to the total real economy is a challenge as much as the challenge of informality itself.

The ratio of listed companies' revenue to GDP using Bloomberg and the IMF's WEO data was 0.3x in both the BRICS and the Bay of Bengal groups in 2016. Groups like BRICS ex China and Pacific Alliance had a higher ratio, while groups like MENA, MINT and East Africa ranked lower. Groups like SAARC, ASEAN and Africa (Big Economies) largely ranked in line with the Bay of Bengal and BRICS. For the countries individually, Thailand had the highest ratio at 0.6x amongst the Bay of Bengal group countries, followed by India at 0.4x, Indonesia and Sri Lanka at 0.2x each and Bangladesh and Vietnam at 0.1x each. Brazil and Mexico ranked close to India, with Russia and the Philippines ranking slightly higher. Turkey, Pakistan and Saudi Arabia ranked close to Indonesia while Nigeria ranked alongside Vietnam. South Korea and South Africa were the leaders in the pack, with ratios at about 1x.

But what is the ideal threshold? Looking at the developed markets under study (i.e. the USA, UK, Canada and Germany) as the threshold, their collective average was ~0.5x. If the Bay of Bengal group's journey from the current 0.3x to the threshold 0.5x indicates the potential opportunity that is left to traverse, then perhaps riding that journey may be an investment opportunity for global portfolio investors.

In conclusion, formalisation of certain business sectors has already received a push in the Bay of Bengal group's markets, as seen from the examples across process, technology and process in the PTP Model. At the same time, formalisation also implies some changes for businesses, and investors have to be wary so that they can identify the right opportunities to target.

Doing vs. Not Doing
The Risk Story

During a trip to Kathmandu in 2016, while chatting with an old lady who owned an eatery in Thamel district, its main tourist drag, the conversation moved from the typical niceties to the things that had made me curious. That entire day, it was easy to spot the Chinese food and household products in several of the shop-fronts, along with the hordes of locals thronging the street-sellers of second-hand woollens around the central area. Chinese products flooding all countries are nothing new. After all, they make the most competitive products in most sectors. However, my curiosity had been aroused by the fact that many of those products in the shops were of food and many of those locals buying second-hand woollens seemed middle-class people. In Indian cities, one would instead find a larger share of low-income migrants buying cheaper woollens from street-sellers. It was the middle-class look of the faces in Kathmandu that compelled me to ask if their purchasing abilities had indeed come down so much. In the case of food, general food products still remain primarily local in most of the regional countries despite the increase in imported packaged foods, as they typically have a shorter shelf-life and so are made with local produce in most cases.

The old lady's account was that income in the peoples' pocket had not kept pace in Nepal in recent years. The cost of everyday items had risen, partly owing to the disruption in the supply of essential products from India to Nepal due to the political agitations at the border earlier that year. Nepal's inflation statistics do show a spike for 2016. The result was that the common-people, including middle-class families, were struggling to manage with their incomes, necessitating many to resort to cheaper street-side woollens and the cheaper Chinese foods. Supply followed demand. In her own business, she said profit margins were reduced. Most of Kathmandu's restaurants and bars are in Thamel district only, and the over-supply of establishments necessitated keeping prices low despite the cost of items going up. She had started her business years ago, and now her children had taken over. The pressure on income meant she still had to work at her age because hiring a new help was not possible, and her children were doing additional businesses to supplement their income. In a country where tourism makes up a large share of economic activity, her experience can be multiplied manifold across such establishments. My question was why she didn't relocate her establishment to another neighbourhood where the supply of restaurants was less, rather than continuing it in Thamel.

Her answer was that the alternative was equally risky! The city may have expanded but tourist spaces have not, since the infrastructure never kept proper pace. Hence, most tourists of the middle-class and budget variety, not just the back-packers, continue to concentrate in the Thamel district, which is not a very big geographical area. So like a vicious circle, most of the new restaurants and bars also continue to come up within this tiny place only, and the resultant over-supply of restaurants in that area has limited one's ability to raise prices in their business, keeping margins under pressure. Since the footfall of such tourists in other areas is too low and uncertain, the prospect of moving one's establishment to another neighbourhood is risky. Those areas also have hotels and restaurants, but those were of the high-end variety catering to wealthier travellers. The majority of the business people of Thamel do not have the level of capital or expertise to compete with that high-end segment. In short, the risk of making a change and not making a change seemed alike.

Data tells a similar story about Nepal. The IMF's WEO data show that Nepal's per capita over the last five years till 2016 has grown the least amongst the South Asian countries. It does share its 5% CAGR with Pakistan and Afghanistan, but those two countries controlled inflation better in the last two years. On a real basis, the Nepalese were left net poorer. Given that the estimate of Nepal's per capita income for the next few years till 2021 is also the lowest amongst all South Asian countries except for the Maldives and Afghanistan, perhaps a near-term reprieve is not yet in sight, and locals will continue to feel the pinch for some time to come.

But the main reason for narrating the old lady's incident was to highlight that sometimes the risk of not doing something (relocation in her case) is as great as the risk of doing something (continuing where she was). In the Bay of Bengal group, it may be pertinent to use that approach as well. Yes, the risks of making a portfolio asset class on yet another acronym, especially one mixing emerging and frontier markets, is fraught with risks. After all, most acronyms in the past have not fulfilled their promise. The other side of the coin is – what is risk of not making a group-approach like this? Investing in an individual market has its own risks in the current economic scenario, which a group-approach across multiple markets can help mitigate to an extent.

The risks of not doing

For a country hopeful to see a revival in its investments that slipped in recent years, the existent high leverage in its system can be bothersome because its savings rate has also dipped in recent years. India had been a high savings country for decades, but it is one of the few emerging markets whose savings rate declined over the last five years; the prominent others being Malaysia and the GCC who were bitten by the trends in global oil prices. Even Brazil and Russia have not slipped as much as India. China is also expected to see a slippage in its savings rate, but it still remains at a very high level. India's savings is still significant in absolute size, but its savings rate is expected to slip. With savings not keeping pace with the demand for investments, it may have no choice but to resort to external borrowings going forward. A higher borrowing outgo will impact its level of fiscal deficit further, which is struggling to stay at 3%. All these may only exacerbate its leverage risk further.

At such a stage, this risk may make it prohibitive to take an exposure to India in one singularly-dedicated portfolio. It may even reduce the investor interest to add new funds dedicated to India, until these fundamentals show decisive improvement. Till that time, a group-approach with countries like Thailand and Indonesia, which are expected to have a surplus of savings over investments and maintain lower leverage, may help mitigate the perception of the risk of a group portfolio vs. that of a singular exposure. The exposure to India is limited within a group portfolio, and such an approach which averages out the risks across countries may evince more interest. Even Vietnam can gain, since it also has a possibility of a slight slippage in its savings rate, which can create pressure on its deficit. Hence, a group approach may aid the perception about Vietnam too. The risk of not doing something, joining a group acronym in this case, may seem as big as the risk of doing something, not joining the acronym.

Can a group-approach impact the perception about the solvency of those economies? A top-down look at the state of these economies today shows a strong case for India to group with its Southeast Asian peers in a portfolio rather than going singular. Back in 2001 when the BRIC term was born, the median number for the percentage of government borrowing to GDP across Russia, China and Brazil was approximately 3% each. India's ratio was more than 3x of this. The leveraged nature of India's economy has continued since then. In 2016, India has a far higher proportion of government borrowing for its economic size than countries like Thailand or Indonesia. Even smaller nations like Nepal and Bhutan have a lower ratio. This has an impact on the perception about the debt challenge in India and the risk of over-leverage that a portfolio singularly dedicated to India may carry vs. that of a group portfolio.

While averaging out ratios within a group portfolio does not really absolve the risk of each country individually, it still indicates the combined risk that fund managers take up in their portfolio whilst investing in multiple markets vs. investing in only one market. From that perspective, India may evince more interest by being part of a group going forward, rather than by itself. Of course, if its savings rate improves, corporate earnings revive and the level of leverage in its economy reduces, and that might change this narrative entirely.

A component-wise Du-Pont analysis of the ROE of Indian companies adds flavour to this. Over the last five years till 2016, the level of debt to equity ratio of the largest 200 listed companies by 2016 market capitalisation has been increasing in India, taking the debt and shareholders' equity of all companies collectively. It is higher than the median figure of over a dozen major emerging economies, and behind only Brazil, Turkey and China. Turkey and Brazil are already facing some heat in the investment community. Egypt, Mexico and Nigeria, which have their own troubles, have also seen an uptick in their ratios but it still remains below this median. On the other hand, Southeast Asian markets like Thailand, Indonesia and Vietnam have either seen their leverage ratios come down or remain flat over this period. Even South Asian markets like Sri Lanka have debt equity ratios lower than India. All of them are part of the Bay of Bengal group. In such a situation, a group-approach may help mitigate the perception of the risk of a group portfolio vs. that of a singular exposure. Yes, one still invests in individual securities, and so the fundamentals of the individual securities matters rather than the collective leverage of the portfolio. Nevertheless, it may help from the perspective of perception of the group's overall leverage.

What is the perception of a group-approach on liquidity? The free-float (total shares less those held by promoters) available to trade in the smaller markets is often less, creating a liquidity risk. The range in the BRICS markets was about 45% collectively in 2017. This figure for the Bay of Bengal group (including for BIMSTEC alone) was about 40%, just a tad below BRICS. The ASEAN had a lower free-float ratio than even the Bay of Bengal group. In the individual countries, this varies from 60–70% in Brazil and South Africa to 40% in China and India each. Amongst the Bay of Bengal group members, the range is concentrated around 40% for most of the larger markets like Thailand, India, Bangladesh and Indonesia. That may be perceived as a positive for a group portfolio since its range is not as divergent here as in the other groups like BRICS.

Liquidity perceptions do not exist only for securities, but also for markets. Fund managers dislike illiquid securities in information-asymmetric markets, unless they are of the adventurous variety studying hard-to-access markets. Most have their own ideas on liquidity; and this can reduce the investible opportunities they are open to. Share trading velocity, as indicated by the World Federation of Exchanges data on average cash equity traded volumes to market capitalisation in their primary exchange, shows a high variation amongst the countries under study. The share trading velocity in the BRICS markets varied from 400%+ in China in 2015, to 100% in Brazil, 45–50% in India and South Africa and down to 35% in Russia. As a group, the BRICS collectively had a trading velocity close to 300%, and 54% on a BRICS ex China basis. It may be pertinent to add that ASEAN and Pacific Alliance had much lower share trading velocities than the Bay of Bengal group. Amongst the markets making up the Bay of Bengal group, Thailand, India and Bangladesh had velocities of 80%, 45% and 40% respectively. The figure for the group collectively was around 50% (including for BIMSTEC alone). That is not far behind the BRICS ex

China grouping. However, since Indonesia, Vietnam and Sri Lanka had a much lower velocity, being part of a group portfolio may evince more interest into those smaller markets than they could have done singularly by themselves.

If one looks at the BRICS in the 2000s, when India had just opened its markets to global portfolio investors and domestic institutions were only starting to pick up, the first wave of inflows to the Indian markets came from global funds. Most of them were group-based funds like emerging market, Asia ex Japan funds or BRICS funds, in which India had a partial allocation. Once the economy started delivering on reforms, business expansion took place in the 2000s. The comfort of the investors deepened; and it opened the door to launch singular-dedicated portfolios to India. In such India-dedicated funds, the allocation to the Indian markets was higher. The domestic institutions eventually developed in the market, incentivised by the vibrancy created by those global investors; they are now reaching a critical mass in assets and clients. In short, a group approach by being part of a portfolio spanning multiple markets helped evince investor interest than what would have been the case had India sat and waited for India-dedicated funds to fructify. Perhaps the push would never have come, because the investors' comfort would not have had an opportunity to be built up irrespective of the performance of the economy. This is more so from the context of India's leverage situation back in 2001, when it was over-leveraged relative to the other BRICS markets.

The risks of doing

Moving from the risks of not doing to the risks of doing, what is the risk for currencies? Does the Bay of Bengal groups risk repeating the 1997 Asian currency crisis, especially since the expectation is that investments will grow in most of these markets in coming years? Or does it risk repeating a BRICS-style slowdown?

Back in 1990s, much of the investments in Southeast Asian markets like Thailand, Indonesia and Malaysia were fuelled by external borrowings and imports, which pushed up the external borrowings and current deficit in the years just before the crisis. These were made on the assumption that the foreign demand for their exports would continue indefinitely. Savings severely lagged behind the high investment rate, necessitating external borrowings. Moreover, the currencies in countries like Thailand were pegged to the US dollar, and as the dollar rose following a weakening of the Japanese yen, so did the Thai baht. Thai exports started losing their competitiveness in the global market. The drop in business, pressure of external debt and exchange rates, and the inability of foreign exchange supply to keep pace, all combined to trigger the Asian currency crisis in 1997.

But the scenario today is different, given the emphasis on financial stability after the crisis. Indonesia, Thailand and Vietnam have a more moderated investment rate today, and their savings rate has risen to amply cover most of it. That has reduced their dependency on external borrowing. South Asian markets like India and Bangladesh have seen their savings rate pick up since the 1990s, despite a recent dip seen in India. Nevertheless, savings still remain large enough to reduce any overt dependency on external borrowings, and the resultant pressure to meet foreign currency debt payments.

In the mid-1990s, the difference between the average savings rate and the average investments rate for the five-years from 1993 to 1997 in Indonesia, Thailand and Malaysia was 600 to 800 base points. This number is expected to reduce to about 200 base points for these countries as well as India, Bangladesh and Sri Lanka for the next five-years from 2016 to 2021, indicating the reducing pressure on external borrowings. In fact, Thailand and Vietnam are expected to see a positive differential.

In the BRICS, headwinds to the commodity trade slowed down the momentum in at least three BRICS members and reduced their relative attraction within investment portfolios. A repeat of this scenario in the Bay of Bengal group is limited since the economic growth drivers of these markets are a fair mix across consumption, investment and exports. This was explained with data in the earlier chapter on Asset Class. In the BRICS, there was some dependence on the commodity export trade in the 2000s. That tilt created a downside risk for the whole BRICS portfolio, once the commodity cycle slumped. In the Bay of Bengal group, a negative impact on one growth driver can be cushioned by the other drivers, thus reducing the overall hit to the portfolio.

This fair mix of consumption, investment and exports may, to some extent, also address the risk that accompanies all acronyms – their ephemeral nature. An acronym's story is getting shorter because the underlying countries are not performing consistently through successive years. For instance, the IMF's WEO data shows that during the first half of the 1980s, half of all economies globally which published their annual GDP numbers clocked a YoY growth rate each year that was higher than the previous year. During the second half of the 1980s, this went up to three-fourths of all economies that published their GDP numbers and further to 80% of all economies during the first half of the 1990s. The second half of the 1990s saw this number come down to two-thirds of all economies. The rising tide effect of the early 2000s saw this rise to as much as 90%, before reducing to a low of only one-third in the year 2009 just after the crisis struck. The early years of the 2010s saw this revive to two-thirds, but the year 2015 again saw it slip to one-third.

With so much wild swings, where can one put one's money with relative certainty of consistent performance? There is a strong case to diversify one's money across economies in an acronym instead of risking in just one economy. What if that one economy saw a continued slowdown and sinks? At least the other boats of the acronym would keep the monies afloat.

One can always narrow down on that one multi-year winning economy, but most analysts have been unable to do that with reasonable accuracy. From 1991 to 2015, only one-fourth of all the economies globally achieved a growth rate higher than the previous year in at least 80% of all years. Unfortunately, this 80%+ list does not include many large emerging markets often quoted in acronyms, except for China, India, Poland, Nigeria, Mexico, Saudi Arabia and Malaysia and the Philippines. Fortunately, this 80%+ list does include markets like India, Bangladesh, Vietnam, Sri Lanka, Myanmar, Nepal and Bhutan, with Thailand and Indonesia closely following at 75% each. All of them are part of the Bay of Bengal group. So while acronyms are ephemeral, the risk of some acronyms may be lesser – and the Bay of Bengal group seems to be one such case!

Finally the political risk; fortunately, most of the Bay of Bengal countries have new leaders at the helm who are making the right noises about reforms, growth, development and stability – be it Narendra Modi in India, Hasina Wajed in Bangladesh, Joko Widodo in Indonesia, Maithripala Sirisena in Sri Lanka, Htin Kyaw and Aung San Suu Kyi in Myanmar or Prayut Chanocha in Thailand. The Heritage Reforms index has gone up in most of these countries recently, and hopefully their momentum to embrace economic change should continue.

In conclusion, there are risks to trying a new step and equal risks of not doing it. This chapter has taken a view of those risks from the perspective of the Bay of Bengal markets, especially the case of India where being part of a group portfolio in its current context of its high leverage and slippage in investment and savings may help mitigate the perception of the risk of a group portfolio vs. that of a singular exposure.

Non-Prerequisites and Enablers
The Integration Story

During a trip to Vietnam in 2017, it was while waiting at Ho Chi Minh City airport for a flight to Hanoi that a cyclone struck. Having finished two university lectures the previous day and two more that morning, reaching Hanoi and getting a good night's sleep was all that mattered to me. So the cyclone could not have struck at a worse time. This storm was an after-effect of the infamous Cyclone Damrey that had struck southern Vietnam, but it was strong enough to throw all the flight schedules off-gear. As all the passengers prepared to bunk the rest of the evening in the airport waiting for the cyclone to pass, the sign-board that flashed the list of flights and timings caught my attention. The list itself showed a long list of delays, but my attention was grabbed by the list of the destinations. My presumption had been the number of cities connected by domestic flights in Vietnam would be limited since it was geographically a small country with only Ho Chi Minh City and Hanoi as the commercial centres. Moreover, it was a socialist country where air travel might be looked upon as a luxury; after all it had been the same situation in India till the early 1990s. This belief was totally wrong! The sign-board listed more than a dozen Vietnamese cities, to where flights were expected to have taken off but were now delayed. That was as many cities as one would see in an airport sign in India at any given time, and India was geographically a much larger country with several commercial centres. Plus, the Indian economy had opened up to privatisation longer than Vietnam. Nothing creates fraternizing bonds as delays in airports or stations; and in a short while some of us got chatting. In the process, an interesting answer came forth from one waiting passenger to my question about Vietnam's air connectivity.

The gentleman was a sales-executive on his way to Da Nang, a town in the middle of Vietnam. His opinion was that the highway connectivity with Thailand and other neighbours pushed road development in Vietnam, and this pushed up airport connectivity. Some years ago, the Thai authorities had approached their neighbours to develop a modern highway network so that freight could move fast, perhaps originally for Thai exports. This need was anyway a dire one since the Khmer Rouge and the Vietnam War had left the region's infrastructure in tatters. Anyway, the highways between Ho Chi Minh City to Phnom Penh and onwards to Bangkok did develop, as did the highways connecting cities within each of these countries. A trip to Cambodia a week later, which included going from Phnom Penh to Siem Reap on that very highway, would remind me of this gentleman's comment. At the time when this regional highway integration was being done, Vietnam faced a practical issue. Vietnam as a country is geographically stretched a long way along its north-south ends while its east-west ends are much narrower; so any road or train travel from end-to-end took a lot of time. So while commerce was picking up in Vietnam, it was not always practically feasible for commercial travellers to spend so many days travelling by highway between Vietnamese cities. So while the highway development improved inter-connectivity, there was an imperative to push other forms of transport within Vietnam, ultimately leading to the development of several airports in the mid-tier towns.

His opinion was that the highway integration pushed the case for developing air connectivity within Vietnam. Had the first not occurred, the flow of commerce may not have increased in a big way. Hence, the authorities may not have found a compelling reason to bother with the second. Commerce had picked up in Vietnam in a big way. The shops and malls in Ho Chi Minh City and Hanoi house as many global brands as their counterparts in India. The airport itself was an example; as the evening progressed, the crowd seemed more typical of the business travellers rather than the typical tourist crowd. It is also a coincidence that the quality of domestic highways is better in Thailand or Cambodia as compared to Vietnam, probably indicating that a part of the resources in Vietnam have had to go into integrating its air connectivity.

This example is reminiscent of the ubiquitous chicken-or-egg story. What came first – the chicken or the egg? Did the highway integration in the region act as the catalyst to develop air integration within Vietnam; after all it helped trade to flow in the first place. Or were Vietnam's airports anyway set to develop on their own because of geographic compulsions and the highway integration merely a coincidence? After all, its government seemed dynamic enough and Vietnam was anyway emerging as the next economic hub in Southeast Asia over the last decade due to domestic drivers like a 90 million plus population, the growing incomes and aspirations of its people, rapid urbanisation and its geographic length. Economic factors would have compelled commerce to flow and the air network to develop for business travellers, irrespective of the highway integration.

Is integration really a precursor?

One can opine what led to what, but this example highlighted an observation — that integration is not always a compulsion for a grouping to function. It is undoubtedly an advantage, but not a compulsion. This means the integration of the highways between the group comprising Thailand, Vietnam and Cambodia was useful. The development of trade and commerce within that group could still have functioned without the modern highway integration given the profile of their economies and development, albeit at a higher cost and longer lag-times. That flow of trade and commerce would still have flown even within Vietnam domestically to feed its growing consumption needs, and would have made a case for integrating its domestic airports with flights for rapid movement of business travellers. In short, Vietnam's airports and domestic air connectivity and the flow of commerce within the regional group need not have depended solely on that modern highway integration. It could still have happened irrespective of it, because there were motivations enough to do so. The highway integration would naturally always have helped, but it was not a compulsion that would hold back other projects and create their dependency on it. This conclusion is debatable. Sub-Saharan Africa makes an interesting analogy, where the lack of modern highway integration between most regional countries does not mean that the flow of commerce is nil. Yes, it flows less than what it should and at a higher cost and lag-time, but it still flows nonetheless. It is an undesirable situation undoubtedly, but it does flow.

Superimposing this thought on the idea of a Bay of Bengal grouping, the question is whether the success of a group asset class idea depends on those markets integrating first, or can it still go ahead without integration?

As said before, integration always helps, but it is not a compulsion. After all, the BRICS group asset class took off in the 2000s without any integration of its financial markets. Even today, a decade and half after Goldman Sachs originally coined the term BRIC, the actual degree of financial (or even trade) integration amongst the BRICS economies remains low. Intra-BRICS trade as a percentage of BRICS GDP has remained only ~3–4% since the last five years (and only ~5–6% on an ex China basis), as per the data in EXIM Bank of India's report 'Intra-BRICS trade: An Indian Perspective'. The Euro currency is at the other end of the spectrum, which involves a holistic integration of the financial markets of each country. Singular markets can still be grouped together in a financial asset class portfolio, and the pieces need not integrate first. Any group asset class idea that spans multiple markets need not require significant integration of their financial markets – that is what makes it a low-hanging fruit.

Of course, efforts towards integration should always be encouraged if it leads to mutually beneficial projects in investment and trade. Trade requires a degree of harmonisation on contentious issues like tariff, quotas and rules for mutual benefit. These negotiations take time as they have to navigate geopolitical hurdles. It makes trade integration a long-gestation project. A group asset class needs less harmonisation because investments are still made to the individual markets; it is just the portfolio basket that is viewed as a whole. That makes it a relatively quick-implementation project as compared to trade negotiations, and ensures that the buzz of the group's story does not die out during the gestation period that trade integration takes. This had helped the BRICS story gain momentum. Had that not happened, perhaps the buzz around BRICS may just have died out in all the time of waiting for deeper trade.

What type of integration might still be useful?

But while integration may be a non-prerequisite for a group asset class idea, it may be pertinent to understand what sort of integration may work out to be enablers for a group asset class. The underlying driver for any financial asset class is that the businesses of that region should prosper, and create value for shareholders in the long term. If businesses flourish, it will have positive ramifications for the economy's demand through job-creation, income, savings and consumption and for the country's supply through production and investment.

From this perspective, RVCs and production migration activities are the most critical for deepening the business sector's prospects in this specific region.

There are three reasons for this. First, the rising cost of labour and real estate elsewhere will drive businesses to search for cheaper areas. People cost and commercial realty rents have risen in the Bay of Bengal group countries as well, but it still remains relatively cheaper than other countries. A simple equation is to see if it feels expensive to buy a cup of tea in a road-side shop in a country? Based on my travels in the regional countries, India, Nepal and Bangladesh felt relatively the cheapest on this front, with Thailand, Malaysia and Sri Lanka at the other end, and Vietnam, Cambodia, Bhutan and Indonesia lying in-between.

Second, migration of production will happen preferably where the global shipping lines lie in close proximity, because these lines will carry the produce to the final market and bring the materials from the suppliers. As such, the Southeast and South Asian countries lie near the shipping lines connecting East Asia with Europe. If geography offers an advantage, this group has it.

Third, RVCs and migration will occur where there are adequate suppliers and ancillary industries available. For example, a computer manufactured in China uses chips made in Taiwan, keyboards made in Malaysia and screens made in South Korea. No one country can possibly have suppliers of all products, although the Bay of Bengal region collectively has quite a few. For instance, a lot of automobile production initially migrated from Japan (and then from South Korea) to the Southeast Asian countries. Now India has built a vibrant automobile spare-parts ancillary industry, to the extent that global auto majors are setting up plants in India for global sourcing – i.e. they not only sell these cars to the Indian market, but they also export them from India to neighbouring countries. Hyundai's plant in Tamil Nadu, a state in southern

India and close to the global shipping lines, is an example. This would not have been possible had India not housed a capable supplier and ancillary network. Similarly, a lot of garment manufacturing is migrating from China to Bangladesh, because Bangladesh has ample supply of cheap, skilled labour as well as adequate cotton imports from India, etc. Even in services, a lot of offshoring work is now migrating from India to Sri Lanka and the Philippines due to talent and cost reasons.

Production migration and RVCs will use a number of suppliers and collaborators spread across the region and link them effectively into the production process. That would give the needed push to the businesses in the group countries, which augurs well for the investors who have bet monies in those businesses. Creating and deepening of new RVC opportunities will be most effective from the context of driving business in this group.

In any case, RVCs and production migration are nothing new. The first phase of migration in manufacturing primarily went from the European countries to the United States in the late 19th century and early 20th century as American enterprises innovated. Then it migrated from the USA to Mexico and Brazil in the 1970s as they emerged as cost-effective places to make products like cars. From the 1980s and 1990s onwards, a tsunami of migration went from the West to China making it the manufacturing superpower. Incidentally, even the iconic London taxi is now made in China. The next phase of migration will primarily occur from China, and the best-placed recipients are the South and Southeast Asian markets, many of whom are part of the Bay of Bengal group.

Suppliers and ancillary industries should be preferably located around the primary factory area, in order for such RVCs to evince maximum currency. In China, many suppliers are located around those cities only. This is one reason why China has seen an explosion of industrial cities, from Tianjin, Beijing in the north, to Dalian, Shanghai in the east and Guangzhou, Shenzhen in the south. Hence, industrial planning has to play a critical role by encouraging clusters based on industries, perhaps through zoning. This includes connectivity of sea and land ports, an area where most South Asian countries still lag behind. This only makes freight transfers more time-consuming and costly, which reduces the chances of cracking RVC deals. If business integration through RVCs cannot happen, it will also diminish the advantage of geographical proximity that this region enjoys. Business integration within a group also means increased networking between business people and people to people (P2P) connection. If a relevant supplier or ancillary can be sourced from a fellow country of the Bay of Bengal group, that would be a win-win for the group. To do this, the businesses first need to have mutual awareness about each other's sectors and markets, then build business relationships with them. Unless networking between businesses deepens, the lack of mutual awareness will remain a challenge for this story.

Even then, geographical proximity is not a necessity

Speaking on geographical proximity; it can be an enabler but again, it is not a prerequisite for a group financial asset class. BRICS was geographically a more disparate group with members spread across continents, yet it saw more portfolio funds than ASEAN – a group of Southeast Asian nations in geographical proximity to each other. What matters more for a financial portfolio asset class is the economic prospects of those countries; hence the stress on their top-down economic stories throughout this book's narrative.

This clicked for BRICS in the 2000s because their economies were in a more homogeneous development profile. Conversely, it has not clicked for ASEAN to that extent as its members became more heterogeneous in their economic profile. Singapore, Malaysia and Brunei are upper-income countries grouped with low-income countries like Laos, Cambodia and Myanmar. The European Union is another case of geographical proximity not contributing to total success. When the European Common Market was originally devised in the 1970s between the six countries of Western Europe that were of a similar economic profile, the group notched one success after another finally leading to the Euro currency. As economically disparate nations from east Europe joined, its degree of success floundered. Members with varied economic profiles mean different priorities, and a portfolio asset class story cannot excel is such an environment. It rather needs the homogeneity of economic profiles and expectations, something BRICS had in the 2000s and the Bay of Bengal group has now.

Even a common cultural history is not a prerequisite for a financial asset class. The Eurozone is connected with the European culture but the BRICS had no cultural or historical links.

In conclusion, integration is always an enabler but it is not a compulsion for a group portfolio asset class idea. Since it does not need much financial integration, it is a low-hanging fruit that can be implemented quickly. Financial integration may not be a compulsion, but an asset class on a group would gain if its business sectors integrate further through regional value-chains or production migration. That should be the topmost agenda for any discussion on integration in this context. Lastly, geographical proximity is not a compulsion either for a group asset class idea, if one compares the success of BRICS and ASEAN on this front.

A Micro-Approach towards Final Outcomes
The Trade Story

During lunch with the faculty head of one of Dhaka's leading business schools whilst on a trip to Bangladesh in 2017, the conversation went on to how Bangladesh is pushing its foreign investment and trade agenda. He explained how the country is pursuing a deal-by-deal approach in specific sectors rather than going the whole-hog across everything. The conversions are happening, especially with the Southeast Asian countries with whom their flow had been low traditionally, but is now slowly rising. They even closed a strategic deal with Cambodia by concentrating in a specific sector, when many others might have assumed making an all-sector push to a commercial hub like Singapore or Malaysia would have been the only norm. Of course, that may have sounded more glamorous for the business dailies covering the event, but the chance of conversion may have been less. Instead, this micro-approach was resulting in a better conversion rate, and that mattered.

This was reminiscent of the many large-scale investor road shows the various provinces of India have been conducting over the last few years. Most of these are macro-events targeting everyone and every sector; and the final conversion of the proposals on the ground is often debatable. Event organizers may show statistics of the participants, meetings and proposals signed; but the real outcome is how effectively the project was finally completed on the ground. Those statistics are often found wanting. That was the difference in Bangladesh's approach, by going by specific deals or sectors and concentrating on those few conversions rather than the initiation. There is a rationale for this approach. The ultimate yardstick is always the outcome. If the final outcome did not happen, there would not be much gain after the initial noise subsided.

While chatting with the faculty head of one of Delhi's policy institutions a few months later the same year, the conversation went to the final outcome of India's imports. In the context of media reports that invariably painted imports as non-essential when India's current account deficit issue flared up in 2012–2013, his view was that it was critical to understand the outcome of imports rather than cliché narratives about imports per se being a cause of concern. Some imports are essential, like capital machinery that help create long term assets and economic value; and which the country cannot produce itself competitively.

Yes, some imports of gold for consumption can always be debated in India's case; but without capital machinery, businesses like telecommunications, etc. would not have taken off in a big way. Such businesses bring in a lot of economic and social value to the nation. Restricting such productive imports would be a cause of concern for national output. The media's cliché narratives aside, it is worth thinking why there is no overt focus of import rules on specific outcomes. Is a more micro-approach to evaluating import's outcomes needed?

While these two anecdotes were set in different contexts, the underlying connect was about taking a more micro-approach with the final outcome in focus, instead of painting the entire canvas in one-colour. This could be in the case of finding trade partners (like in Bangladesh's example) or in identifying needed imports (like in India's example).

Has India's trade story gained by being a part of the BRICS group?

Let us put this in the context of India's trade story while being a part of the BRICS. The country has been a part of the BRICS grouping for over a decade but what has really been the final outcome for India's trade story? Consider the case of imports, something which has been under the media's glare since the current account deficit issue in 2012–2013. Does the final outcome of India's trade story with the BRICS, as it stands now, merit a more micro-focus on specific sectors and purposes?

As per the data in Indian Commerce Ministry's commodity-wise export-import data bank, the specific outcome of asset-creating productive imports has been satisfied only in the case of India's imports from China – just one nation out of the lot. In the fiscal year 2016–2017, India imported ~US$33 billion of electrical machineries and mechanical appliances from China, the highest it sourced for this purpose from any BRICS country. In the first six months of 2017–2018, this had already crossed ~US$20 billion. Even amongst the other import categories with China, there are some products like chemicals, accessories, metals, etc. that can also be partially described as asset-creating. All these items made up as much as two-thirds of India's imports with China: an asset-creating outcome. This final outcome may have been met because India and China often conduct sector specific trade-fairs and industrial events; is this a benefit to a more micro-approach to target manufacturers of specific machineries?

But an asset-creating final outcome does not seem to have occurred in India's imports with the other BRICS countries. With Russia, India's largest import was precious metals and stones in the same year. This is mainly used in the jewellery industry for private final consumption, rather than productive asset-creation. Moreover, this flow has only grown between 2016–2017 and 2017–2018.

With South Africa, precious metals and stones comprised one-third of India's imports. With Brazil, sugar comprised one-fourth of India's imports. These two products are mainly used respectively in the jewellery and confectionary industries for private final consumption, rather than productive asset-creation. There are other categories on India's import list with these countries, but none seems to be a significantly asset-creating one.

Considering that BRICS has been a key story since the last decade, India should have channelled the final outcome of that relationship more into productive needs; and investment in asset-creation does remain a core need. So would a micro-approach to deepening its trade with specific outcomes in mind help serve it better; that is the question to be asked at this juncture?

In fact, the entire BRICS trade story raises questions, not just India's piece within it. As per the data in EXIM Bank of India's report 'Intra-BRICS trade: An Indian Perspective', intra-BRICS trade as a proportion to the BRICS GDP was ~3% in 2006, when the group was formalised by the governments. It was still at ~3% in 2015, a decade later. Even the intra-BRICS trade to total BRICS trade held flat at ~8–10% through this decade. Intra-regional trade did not grow disproportionately as a result of the grouping. Yes, the proportion of intra-BRICS trade to GDP did touch 4.5% during 2009, just before the cyclical and structural challenges took hold in some of the member countries. That did not sustain. Perhaps a more micro, outcome-based approach might have helped replace the trade of some products that the BRICS members did with other countries with fellow BRICS members themselves; thus deepening the trade flows dispropor-tionately within the group. If that never occurred, what was the advantage to the trade story by being part of a group?

Did the BRICS grouping exacerbate India's deficit problem?

This debate about the BRICS trade story also extends to India's deficit situation; something that got the media excited a few years ago. As per the data of the IMF's WEO and the EXIM Bank of India report, the GDP of the BRICS nations collectively grew at a 12% CAGR during the decade from 2006 to 2015 while intra-BRICS trade also grew at a 12% CAGR. Hence, its ratio held constant. Within this, the growth of both export volumes and import volumes were similar. But these numbers are for the BRICS collectively.

India's own trade within intra-BRICS trade also grew at a 12% CAGR in this period, but the growth of its exports was only 4%. So while its intra-BRICS trade did pick up, most of it was in imports; that too with non-productive consumption creating imports comprising a fair share of its imports with the BRICS ex China group countries (Brazil, Russia and South Africa). In the process, its trade deficit grew from ~US$9 billion in 2005 to ~US$60 billion by 2015. The widest gap in this trade deficit occurred from 2013 to 2015, when India's import share within the BRICS ex China grouping's imports picked up from 34% to 44% while its share within the BRICS ex China group's exports dipped from 21% to 17%.

As India anyway runs an overall trade deficit, the imbalance between its import share vs. export share with the BRICS ex China countries only applied further pressure on the country's current account deficit. Consumption is not a bad thing; in fact it is a key driver of economic growth which has often eluded export-oriented nations in economic history. Nevertheless, carrying a recurring foreign exchange and current account deficit pressure just to drive consumption is probably taking it too far. Conversely, an asset-creating import is an investment which would ideally realize some productive value and returns over the long term, thus compensating for the current deficit pressure to some extent.

There is a caveat; when the acronym BRIC was first coined in 2001, the share of BRICS (including South Africa) in India's imports was ~6%, while the share of BRICS in India's exports was ~5%. The proportion of imports only travelled north since then, while exports turned south. So the final outcome for India remains debatable.

India's trade with the Bay of Bengal group countries

Turning to India's trade profile with the countries of the Bay of Bengal group, the share of these countries within India's total imports in 2017 was ~7%, as per the data in Indian Commerce Ministry's commodity-wise export-import data bank. The share of these countries within India's exports is higher at ~11%. India did have a trade deficit with Indonesia and Thailand in 2016–2017 of a similar amount as with the BRICS ex China countries. It had a trade surplus with Vietnam, Myanmar, Bangladesh and Sri Lanka. From the perspective of deficit, the arithmetic looks better! So its trade with the Bay of Bengal group compares more favourably than the BRICS ex China group from the perspective of trade imbalance, despite over a decade of the BRICS story.

Moreover, the share of the Bay of Bengal countries within India's total trade now is already higher than the share of the BRICS in 2001. As of 2017, the value of India's goods exports to Brazil or Russia each was less than its exports to each of the Bay of Bengal markets like Bangladesh, Indonesia, Thailand, Vietnam and Sri Lanka. At the same time, the value of India's goods imports from Brazil, Russia or South Africa each is as high as its imports from each of the Bay of Bengal markets like Bangladesh, Indonesia, Thailand, Vietnam and Sri Lanka. In short, the Bay of Bengal trade story is as significant, or possibly more, for India as the BRICS ex China trade story was, and a further push will only deepen this further.

On a product basis, over one-third of India's imports from Thailand were electrical machineries and mechanical appliances during 2016–2017, as per the data in Indian Commerce Ministry's commodity-wise export-import data bank. These are the same categories that comprised most of its imports from China. Similarly, over one-third of India's imports from Vietnam were electrical machineries and mechanical appliances. Its imports from the other group countries had a lesser share of asset-creating categories, and were more concentrated on materials and agro-produce. The exact machinery products imported from China, Thailand and Vietnam may be different and may not necessarily be replaceable with each other; but there is still some tilt towards the outcome of focusing on asset-creating imports. So can some of the machineries imported from China be replaced by Thailand or Vietnam, thus pushing complementarities in trade amongst the Bay of Bengal countries?

Or are unnecessary tariffs or quotas making Thai or Vietnamese imports uncompetitive relative to China, in cases where the machineries are similar? Trade negotiation activities of the BIMSTEC (and Bay of Bengal grouping) have to address these product-issues with a micro-approach. That would help the trade outcome immensely.

Vehicles formed ~8% of India's combined exports to the countries forming the BRICS, Bay of Bengal and South Asian groups in 2017, the second-largest item after petrochemicals. Deeper trade linkages may help drive this further, especially in the commercial vehicle segment which indirectly contributes towards asset-creation outcomes. Indian tuk-tuks are sold in Jakarta and Colombo; this should be expanded to more vehicle formats. Pharmaceuticals contribute towards worker productivity, so can indirectly impact asset-creation. However, it forms only ~4% of India's combined exports to these countries. Deeper trade linkages may drive this further with the group countries. Bangladesh is the world's second-largest manufacturer of readymade garments after China, exporting to several countries. Over 40% of India's cotton export goes to Bangladesh, from amongst these countries combined. As Bangladesh sees traction in its garment industry due to export deals and migration from Chinese factories, it gives reason for India to ramp up its supply of raw cotton further, rather than let suppliers like Egypt take away that incremental business.

Global sourcing in manufacturing is an opportunity in regional trade, especially when geographic proximity is an advantage. It means a foreign investment to open a factory in another country, from where the product can then be exported to markets around that region. The regional perspective plays a key role in global sourcing. It contributes to the investment rate in the recipient country, while employing workers which has its multiplier-effect. For instance, South Korea's Hyundai invested in an Indian factory, from where it exports cars elsewhere.

Too much trade dependency can be a bad thing

Excessive trade dependency is a challenge. In the BRICS story of the 2000s, there was some dependency on the commodity trade. This dependency was more acute for commodity-exporters like Brazil, Russia and South Africa, than for commodity importers like China. The Chinese demand for commodities was much larger in comparison to exporters like Brazil, Russia and South Africa. As per country-wise foreign trade data of the World Bank's World Integrated Trade Solutions (WITS), only 7% of China's total imports came from the BRICS countries in 2015. The share of China's imports within intra-BRICS imports was much higher at 40%, as per the data in EXIM Bank of India's report 'Intra-BRICS trade: An Indian Perspective'.

Hence, if the demand from one nation determines the trade of another to a large extent, then it can be a challenge. This was the situation for Brazil, Russia and South Africa. What is the scenario for the Bay of Bengal countries?

As per the World Bank's WITS data, 60% of Nepal's imports came from India and 63% of its exports went to India in 2015. So Nepal's trade with India is a big deal, although India's trade with Nepal was only 10% of its total trade with the Bay of Bengal countries. Similarly, 80% of Bhutan's imports came from India and 90% of its exports went to India. India's trade with Bhutan is only 1% of its total trade with the Bay of Bengal countries. Again, it is a bigger deal for Bhutan. So the risk appreciates in these two relationships.

But this risk may be lower in other cases. For Bangladesh, 12% of its imports came from India while 5% came from Indonesia. For Sri Lanka, 22% of its imports came from India while 3% came from Thailand. 7% of Sri Lanka's exports went to India. For Myanmar, 12% of its imports came from Thailand, 4% came from Indonesia and 3% came from India, while 27% and 8% of its exports went to Thailand and India respectively. So the risk may be slightly higher only in the India-Sri Lanka and Thailand-Myanmar relationships.

For Indonesia, 8% of its imports came from Thailand, while 8% and 4% of its exports went to India and Thailand respectively. For Thailand, 3% of its imports came from Indonesia, while 4% of its exports went to Indonesia and Vietnam each followed by 2% to India. In Vietnam, 5% and 2% of its imports came from Thailand and India respectively. So the degree of dependency is far less in these relationships.

Unfortunately, ensuring trade relationships are optimal and do not create untoward dependencies are easier said than done. Producing competitive products is only one aspect of successful trade. Closing the long-gestation negotiations over tariff and quotas for mutual benefit is another ball-game, as is the overall political economy that can create an enabling environment. As far as the BIMSTEC is concerned (and also amongst the broader Bay of Bengal group countries), the support from the political economy is there. These governments are working on trade discussions which should be leveraged to create competitive opportunities for business, ultimately making the case for investors in those businesses and for a financial asset class on this grouping. Using a more micro-approach with the final outcome of asset-creation in mind may help deepen the trade ties for more long term benefits, coming back to the anecdotes mentioned earlier in this chapter.

At the same time, the intention of this final chapter is not to deride the BRICS trade story, especially the BRICS ex China trade with India. Trade for consumption remains important, as does trade for asset-creation. The moot objective to highlight the profile of the BRICS ex China trade with India is to stress that given India's stage of evolution and the imperative to push growth, an asset-creating objective in its imports may be better. Hence, a micro-approach with this final outcome in mind may be a better alternative at this juncture.

In conclusion, intra-regional trade is not a necessity for a financial asset class idea. The BRICS story grew despite its intra-regional trade story not seeing a disproportionate uptick. At the same time, a micro-approach with the final outcome in mind can be more beneficial, and it is critical to ensure that the deepening of trade in a group does not exacerbate the deficit problem. The trade relationships for India within the Bay of Bengal countries are already on a better footing than the BRICS. Trade stories take time to action, and only now does it seem to be moving in the BRICS. Since an asset class story does not really need intra-regional trade to be a precursor, it can be implemented quickly – making it an ideal low-hanging fruit!

Conclusion

The world has seen, and will always see, the creation of regional groups to converge common interests in trade, investments and geopolitics. Unlike trade and economic blocs, a grouping for a portfolio asset class idea is a quicker implementation project - making it a low-hanging fruit. However, it presupposes that there is adequate awareness and appreciation amongst the financial economy about that group. If there is a gap in the awareness and appreciation, the initial buzz will not be created about that group and the financial community may be unable to complement the political economy's efforts to the extent desired.

The Bay of Bengal grouping (an extension of BIMSTEC) is one such example being proposed in this book. Its chapters compare the top-down economic and corporate performance of this group's markets with other peer markets and regions, in order to trigger the initial awareness and appreciation of the group. That would help them appreciate the potential of these economies, their homogeneity, complementarities, and conceiving them as a cohesive group. The eventual objective is to push the rationale to set up a portfolio asset class on this group, just like it occurred in the BRICS when its buzz spread in the early 2000s. That could eventually lead the way for creating portfolio funds dedicated to this group, just like a plethora of BRIC-dedicated funds saw inception during the 2000s. Going by the experience of those BRICS funds, Bay of Bengal funds could result in more inflows into the local markets than what would have been possible into them otherwise.

The previous chapters have shown why the drivers of economic growth in the Bay of Bengal group are a fair mix; the commonalities and complementarities of the group's economies; relative profit performance of their companies and how the group stands out on this metric; the savings and purchasing power comparisons; the sector-mix, which seems in line with the experience of matured markets; how formalisation is creating deeper business opportunities; intra-group trade equation; the group's potential contribution from productivity, and much more. The narrative has also stressed why it is to India's advantage to be part of a group like this, despite its relatively larger size. While each of the chapters has dealt with a separate theme, together they add up to show the rationale for this grouping.

I am confident that the arguments and data put forward will generate investor interest in these countries as a single group. Deeper investor interest would make the markets more vibrant, and that augurs well to create a motivating ecosystem for corporates and entrepreneurs. For global businesses, it can be the next big marketing campaign, just like the BRICS was.

Bibliography

Daily Star, 'Forget SAARC: Think BIMSTEC' [web page], http://www.thedailystar.net/frontpage/forget-Saarc-think-Bimstec-1294333, (accessed September 2017).

JP Morgan Blogs, 'Hitting the "BRIC" Wall: What's next for EM?' [web page], https://blog.jpmorganinstitutional.com/2015/03/hitting-the-bric-wall-whats-next-for-em/, (accessed December 2017).

South Asia Monitor, 'BIMSTEC a better regional cooperation option than SAARC' [web page] http://southasiamonitor.org/detail.php?type=sl&nid=10234, (accessed September 2017).

Indian Express, 'BIMSTEC in BRICS: A mini-SAARC summit in the making' [web page], http://indianexpress.com/article/india/india-news-india/Bimstec-in-Brics-3085375/, (accessed September 2017).

Stock Exchange of Thailand, 'SET Index Series' [web page], https://market-data.set.or.th/mkt/sectorialindices.do?language=en&country=US, (accessed September 2017).

Statista, 'Share of Apple's revenue by geographical region' [web page], https://www.statista.com/statistics/382288/geographical-region-share-of-revenue-of-apple/, (accessed December 2017).

Women in Informal Employment: Globalizing and Organizing, 'Rethinking Formalisation: The WIEGO Perspective' [web page], http://www.wiego.org/informal-economy/rethinking-formalisation-wiego-perspective, (accessed November 2017).

Live Mint, 'Formalizing India's informal economy' [web page], http://www.livemint.com/Opinion/4kxau3CejBat9uAIEakIKK/Formalizing-Indias-informal-economy.html, (accessed November 2017).

Live Mint, 'Moving towards a larger formal economy' [web page], http://www.livemint.com/Opinion/KVS6qozgENxulaVcFOW0qL/Moving -towards-a-larger-formal-economy.html, (accessed November 2017).

Bloomberg Quint, 'Towards A More Formal Indian Economy' [web page], https://www.bloombergquint.com/business/2017/02/14/towards-a-more-formal-indian-economy-a-conversation-with-v-anantha-nageswaran, (accessed November 2017).

Bloomberg Quint, 'A 'Jhatka' To Push Formalisation In The Economy Could Come At A Cost: Raghuram Rajan' [web page], https://www.bloombergquint.com/business/2017/09/08/a-jhatka-to-push-formalisation-in-the-economy-could-come-at-a-cost-raghuram-rajan, (accessed November 2017).

Kotak Securities, 'Economy to see multi-year benefits from formalisation' [web page], https://m.dailyhunt.in/news/india/english/investment+guru+india-epaper-invgur/economy+to+see+multi+year+benefits+from+formalisation+kotak+sec-newsid-75719668, (accessed November 2017).

The Dawn, 'Taking the banking sector to the next level' [web page], http://aurora.dawn.com/news/1141552, (accessed December 2017).

EXIM Bank, 'Intra-BRICS trade: An Indian Perspective' [web page], https://www.eximbankindia.in/Assets/Dynamic/PDF/Publication-Resources/ResearchPapers/80file.pdf, (accessed October 2017).

The Hindu, 'BRICS nations should trade more in each other's currency' [web page], http://www.thehindu.com/business/Economy/BRICS-nations-should-trade-more-in-each-other's-currency-says-India/article16070237.ece, (accessed November 2017).

Business Insider, 'BRICS MINT CIVETS: Acronym Investing' [web page], www.businessinsider.com/bric-mint-civets-acronym-investing-2014-1, (accessed November 2017).

Tralac, 'Intra-BRICS trade: An Indian Perspective' [web page], https://www.tralac.org/news/article/10701-intra-brics-trade-an-indian-perspective.html, (accessed December 2017).

SIT Journal of Management, 'India-Thailand Trade Relations: An Assessment' [web page], https://www.slideshare.net/bhopal39/india-thailand-trade-relation, (accessed December 2017).

Russia Beyond, 'Intra-BRICS trade has a long way to g' [web page], https://www.rbth.com/economics/business/2016/10/17/intra-brics-trade-has-a-long-way-to-go_639469, (accessed December 2017).

Central Bank of Sri Lanka, 'Annual Report: Economic and Social Infrastructure' [web page], http://www.cbsl.gov.lk/pics_n_docs/10_pub/_docs/efr/annual_report/AR2012/English/7_Chapter_03.pdf, (accessed December 2017).

Department of Statistics Malaysia, 'Labour Force & Social Statistics' [web page], https://www.dosm.gov.my/v1/index.php?r=column/ctwoByCat&parent_id=123&menu_id=U3VPMldoYUxzVzFaYmNkWXZteGduZz09, (accessed December 2017).

WITS World Integrated Trade Solutions, 'Product Exports By Country and Region' [web page], https://wits.worldbank.org/CountryProfile/en/Country/BTN/Year/2012/TradeFlow/Export/Partner/all/Product/Total, (accessed November 2017).

The Heritage Foundation, 'Index of Economic Freedom' [web page], http://www.heritage.org/index/explore?view=by-variables, (accessed December 2017).

National Stock Exchange of India, 'Business Growth in CM Segment' [web page], https://www.nseindia.com/products/content/equities/equities/historical_equity_businessgrowth.htm, (accessed October 2017).

Yahoo Finance, 'World Indices data' [web page], https://in.finance.yahoo.com/world-indices, (accessed September 2017).

IMF data, 'IMF World Economic Outlook Database' [web page], https://www.imf.org/external/pubs/ft/weo/2017/01/weodata/index.aspx, (accessed September 2017).

CEIC Euromoney, 'China Market Capitalisation: Shanghai Stock Exchange' [web page], https://www.ceicdata.com/en/indicator/china/data/market-capitalisation-shanghai-stock-exchange-marketable, (accessed October 2017).

World Bank, 'International Debt Statistics' [web page], http://datatopics.worldbank.org/debt/ids/country/CHN, (accessed November 2017).

Commerce Ministry, Government of India, 'Commodity-wise – Export Import Data Bank' [web page], http://commerce.gov.in/eidb/Icntcom.asp, (accessed January 2018).

Financial Times, 'The story of the Brics' [web page], https://www.ft.com/content/112ca932-00ab-11df-ae8d-00144feabdc0, (accessed January 2018).

ILO, 'Labour productivity – ILO modelled estimates' [web page], http://www.ilo.org/ilostat/faces/oracle/webcenter/portalapp/pagehierarchy/Page3.jspx?MBI_ID=49, (accessed January 2018).

CIA Factbook, 'GDP Composition by End Use' [web page], https://www.cia.gov/library/publications/the-world-factbook/fields/print_2259.html, (accessed March 2018).

Ministry of Statistics, Government of India, 'BRICS joint Statistical Publication 2016' [web page], http://www.mospi.gov.in/sites/default/files/publication_reports/BRICS_JSP_2016.pdf, (accessed April 2018).

Index